Two Weak Women
and
Amazing Grace

To Bonnie
 With our best wishes
that you will always seek
His highest and best.

 Bonnie Hanson

1 Cor. 1:27-29

Two Weak Women AND Amazing Grace

Bonnie J. Hanson

Faith Ventures, Inc.
Fellowship Valley Retreat
1212 Bear Gap Rd. Clarkesville, GA. 30523
Phone: 706-754-4804; Int'l Students: 706-754-4166
Email: faven@hemc.net

Two Weak Women
Copyright © 1996, 2001
Faith Ventures, Inc.

Cover and text illustrations by Bonnie J. Hanson.

All rights reserved. No part of this publication may be reproduced, stored in a retrieval system, or transmitted in any form or by any means—electronic, mechanical, photocopying, recording, or otherwise—without the prior written permission of the publisher and copyright owners.

Printed in the United States of America.

ISBN 09662183-0-2

Dedication

"To God be the glory,
great things He hath done."

Contents

Prologue	9
1. Two Weak Women	13
2. The Astonishing Answer	21
3. A Life-Changing Dream	25
4. Like The Eagles	33
5. The Big Leap	37
6. The University of "Hard Knocks"	43
7. Joy At The Midnight Hour	47
8. Amazing Grace!	53
9. The Baffled Weatherman	59
10. The Blessings of Obedience	61
11. Help!!	65
12. "When I Am Weak"	79
13. A Merry Heart	91
14. Deer Never Cry "Help!"	99
15. You're On The Air!	103
16. An Incredible Deal	111
17. Transparent As Cooking Onions	115
18. To The Ends Of The Earth	127
19. The Storm Of The Century	135
20. Encompassed By Angels	139
21. Deluges!!	145
22. The Lord's Unique Building Plan	149
23. The Fingerprints of God	165
24. Lord, Give Us This Mountain!	177

Prologue

There is a spiritual secret that is little mentioned in today's preaching and teaching. It is summed up briefly in the Lord's words, "My thoughts are not your thoughts, neither are your ways my ways" (Isaiah 55:8). What *are* some of these thoughts and ways that are of the Lord and not of the natural mind? (1) "My strength is made perfect in weakness. Most gladly therefore will I rather glory in my infirmities, that the power of Christ may rest upon me . . . for when I am weak, then am I strong" (2 Corinthians 12:9–10). (2) "But God hath chosen the foolish things of the world to confound the wise; and God hath chosen the weak things of the world to confound the things which are mighty; And base things of the world, and things which are not, to bring to nought things that are: that no flesh should glory in His presence" (1 Corinthians 1:27–29). The Holy Spirit has personalized this truth to my co-worker, Alline Marshall, and to me in a special way as we have taken steps to follow Him in ventures which could only be thought ridiculous in the natural. As two very weak women, we have been given the rare privilege of "stepping out on the seeming void and finding the Rock beneath." We are not unusual people, just those to whom God granted a special delight of seeing Him work out His ways in human situations and circumstances. He gladly leads and reveals Himself and His ways to anyone who is willing to follow Him at all cost. What an adventure we would have missed if we had not followed His leading! What revelations of His character and grace we would have missed if we had not allowed Him to take us into impossible situations where we could witness His power and love at work. He waits to show Himself to any who truly seeks to follow Him with an open heart. To that one He will reveal the secrets of His ways.

When we understand that it is only as we recognize our own utter weakness that we can see the Lord demonstrate His power, then are we partakers in a special secret. When we see at last that He deliberately *chooses* weak and foolish instruments, then we will not worry about powerful programs and rich, financial backers as we step out to serve the Lord. We don't even need to know God's whole plan at the outset. For after all, He holds the schedule and program of each day, month, and year in His hands, and He will reveal His plan to us at the appropriate moment. Our part is to pray and wait for His time for the next step. But waiting is one of the most difficult tasks of the Christian life. We have been taught by our pressured, success-oriented, and highly commercialized society that to succeed we need years of training, the latest equipment, and plenty of finances. And success to the natural mind is very important, for we need to report our achievements to our supporters so that funds will continue to flow in.

But who of us has the time to sit and wait on God when emergencies and financial stresses are upon us? We would rather discover a formula or technique for reaching our goal quickly than take the time to wait patiently for God to reveal His plan. But ideas of formulas and techniques come from the secular mind, not from the spiritual mind, for God cannot be captured in a formula. He has a glorious way of breaking out of our constricting programs, definitions, and plans. "For as the heavens are higher than the earth, so are my ways higher than your ways, and my thoughts than your thoughts" (Isaiah 55:9). We may struggle to do the work of God by our own strength, our own cleverness, our own natural talents and

Prologue

skills. But when we finally fall down exhausted by our efforts and turn to Him, then we will see, at last, that our failure results from disregarding His ways and His principles. Paul, that highly educated man who finally fell on his face before the Lord, learned this secret. He said, "When I am weak, then am I strong . . ." (2 Corinthians 12:9–10). God does indeed choose the weak vessels "that no flesh may glory in His presence."

The wonderful works of the Lord which you will find unfolded in these pages are our testimony of joy in being His weak vessels. The story of what He has already done is told here, but the story is still unfolding. We are still "walking on the water" with Him, pressing on to see Him fulfill all the amazing plans He has for us and for this ministry. We can testify that you, too, can have the breathtaking delight of walking with Him in a miraculous mode of life. This experience of trusting Him for everything can and should be our daily walk if we are obedient and conscious of Him in the details of our circumstances. God is *always* at work to meet us in our needs. But too often we are so rushed, so pressured, and perhaps so distraught, that we fail to recognize His hand at work. We suddenly see "daylight" in the darkness of our need, and we attribute it to mere happenstance that the answer came. Rather, we need to acknowledge Him in the details and then we will be able to delight in the wonder of the final BIG deliverance that He works for us.

We saw His working in so many small ways in our ventures of faith, and those small ways were part of the larger pattern. How we marveled as we saw, at last, what He had been working toward!

As we have trusted Him for miracles, we have learned priceless lessons of faith in Him regarding timing, finances, relationships, and the unfolding of *His* will. Unbelief will rob us of experiencing His power and purposes in our lives. "Those who trust Him wholly, find Him wholly true," the old hymn says. And we say, "AMEN."

1

Two Weak Women

There she was, a Phi Beta Kappa graduate of one of the finest women's colleges in the nation, a microbiologist who taught botany at Barnard College at Columbia University in New York City. And here she was sitting at the edge of a hole filled with sloppy, red clay and water! Her feet were in the mud, and so was she. If only her Agnes Scott friends could have seen her in this state. She looked like a lady mud wrestler, smeared and splattered, yet she appeared to be actually *enjoying* it.

This was the *new* Alline Marshall, launched on her unparalleled career as chief maintenance man at Fellowship Valley. Though a novice might not have realized it, Alline was doing a *plumbing* job! An underground waterline had burst, and water bubbled merrily to the surface like a new spring. Alline dug up the site around the break and then began the repair work. With scientific technique and determination (plus tips she had learned by watching over the shoulder of various plumbers who had worked for us), she fitted the new parts into the broken connection. Then she neatly tightened the screws on the clamps, and the job was done! The flow of water was restored to various buildings. We discovered over the years that breaks like this one usually occurred just before a retreat group was due to arrive, or some other event was about to take place!!

Maintenance work was a great training ground for Alline. Her favorite verse is: "In everything give thanks, for this is the will of God in Christ Jesus concerning you" (1 Thessalonians 5:18). She has had many opportunities to put that verse into practice as she has learned to be our maintenance man!

This faith venture all started innocently enough—two women coming from normal backgrounds, each pursuing plans that seemed natural to her individual talents and skills. But then the Lord stepped in, and life was never the same for Alline Marshall and Bonnie Hanson!

After college, Alline had gone on to do her post-graduate work at various schools, such as Columbia University where she earned her Master's degree, the University of Georgia, and finally Emory University. She worked at Atlanta's Center For Disease Control where she was engaged in leprosy research. She also studied cancer research techniques at Sloan-Kettering Institute in New York City and taught botany at Barnard College in Manhattan. She moved on to Mary Baldwin College in Staunton, Virginia, where she taught botany and microbiology and then began to pursue her doctorate at Emory in the field of microbiology.

She was nearing the end of that arduous task when the Lord intervened in her life, bringing a change of direction. She had developed a degenerate disc in her back and was in such pain that she could no longer lean over a microscope. Eventually, she could no longer bear the pain and had to lay down her plans for obtaining the doctoral degree.

She returned home to south Georgia in such agony that, to put it in her words, she was "nearly climbing the wall with pain." Surgery offered no help. She was hemmed in by her painful disability. Then one day the Lord said to her, "You know, you have never *thanked* me for this pain." Alline was taken aback by this thought, but she quickly realized the truth of it. She had *not* thanked Him. So she began to do so, a bit feebly at first. She could only bring herself to utter thanks with her lips, not with her heart. But as time went on, she found praise and thanksgiving arising from her heart to the Lord. The Lord graciously responded with His touch on her physical body, and the healing began. It was not an instant healing, but over a period of time it became obvious that God had indeed done something very wonderful for her.

She volunteered to serve for a short time at a Bible-correspondence ministry called The Mailbox Club in Valdosta, Georgia. She intended to stay a month but remained for four years.

Then the Lord spoke to her again, calling her in 1970 into C.L.C. (Christian Literature Crusade), a foreign mission headquartered near Philadelphia. There she was placed in the publishing department to do editorial proofreading on book manuscripts. In 1974, Alline took steps of obedience to follow the Lord's leading to the Philippine Islands.

The natural man, looking at the highly educated and well-trained Alline, who had forsaken alluring opportunities in the world of science and teaching, would have asked, "Why this waste?" But the Lord never wastes anything, much less a life poured out as a love offering to Him. He takes the offering and causes the sweet perfume of it to fill the house and far beyond, to touch lives and bring others to commitment to Christ.

A small Iowa town, flanked by farms and vast corn fields, was my birthplace and home. Born with a defective heart, I found myself confined to bed for long periods of time during my childhood. Both my doctor and my mother held me back from vigorous activities, but I did manage to escape at times into a vacant lot nearby to pitch for the neighborhood baseball team! Mostly, however, my world was like Longfellow's description in his poem, "The Land of Counterpane," in which a sick child plays with his toys among the quilts on his bed.

Sometimes the Lord gives special gifts to make up for things one lacks in certain areas. Such was the case in my life.

I was blessed with gifts in art and writing which helped to fill my days.

After graduating from high school, I briefly attended an art school in Minneapolis. It was here that the Lord stepped into my life in a significant way. Members of the Inter-Varsity Christian Fellowship chapter invited me to their meetings, and the home in which I roomed turned out to be a Christian home. The Lord had me neatly cornered, and I soon came to know Him as my Lord and Savior.

I was introduced to a Bible school, Bethany College of Missions , and felt led of God to enroll there. During my three years of training, I received a call to work with the mission agency, Christian Literature Crusade. I initially thought my call was to an overseas post in the West Indies in one of the mission's book centers, but the Lord had other plans for me.

In 1955 I began candidate training with the mission. Apart from the practical duties, which all candidates were given, I was assigned to work in the art department of the printshop. When I finished my candidate time, I became editor of the mission's magazine, *Floodtide*. I also designed book jackets, brochures, and various other publicity materials which the mission printed. I helped represent the mission at conferences and assisted in the orientation of candidates coming into C.L.C.

For nearly twenty years I served in this ministry to the world as a staff worker at the mission headquarters. I thought the rest of my life would be spent right there, but the Lord had a surprise awaiting me.

As mentioned before, in 1970 Alline became a part of Christian Literature Crusade and soon joined the publishing department. During this time we didn't come to know each other very well, since we attended different churches and had different circles of friends. After three years at the U.S. headquarters, Alline received a call to a short term of service in the Philippines with C.L.C. Her job was to transpose British and American books into simplified English for Asians who used English as a secondary language. The books were printed on our mission presses in the Philippines and distributed to various parts of Asia.

I volunteered to produce her prayer letter and send it out while she was overseas. We didn't realize it then, but the Lord probably arranged this to keep a link between us.

It was after Alline left for the Philippines that I began to sense that my time at the mission was coming to a close. My roots were deep in the work, so the thought of leaving was very traumatic for me. A missionary friend called me one day and said that the Lord had given her a word for me from the Scriptures. It was Isaiah 43:19, "Behold I will do a new thing; now it shall spring forth; shall ye not know it?" This and other Scriptures that God gave to me during those months encouraged me as I took steps to resign. I didn't know what the Lord had planned for me. I was physically the weakest of vessels. During my years at the mission, my heart problem had been diagnosed, and I had undergone open-heart surgery to close the holes inside my heart. But I was still frail.

The confirmation of my decision to leave came in late 1974. At that time the Lord strongly impressed upon me that Alline and I should work together in the future. I had no idea what Alline would think of that. We scarcely knew each other. Nevertheless, after I resigned I wrote to her in the Philippines and told her of this strong impression that I felt the Lord had given me. She wrote back immediately saying that the Lord had told her the same thing. She had said to the Lord, "Lord, I am not going to say anything to Bonnie about this. If this is of you, then you have her write to me about it." Within a week my letter arrived telling her of the Lord's word to me. In that same time frame, Alline received a letter from a prayer partner in Georgia, in which she said, "I wonder if the Lord would have you and Bonnie work together...." We felt that the Lord was saying something definite to us, so we began to pray about this possibility.

What could two women DO as a ministry? As we prayed and considered this, we came to the conclusion that God would have us teach the Word. We had both visited many kinds of churches over the years, and we knew that there were many people faithfully going to church each Sunday who were receiving little more than the basic message of John 3:3, "Ye must be born again." We also knew that Christians needed the "meat" of the Word if they were to grow. They needed to hear about death to self and a new, victorious life in Christ. They should be thriving and growing in their understanding of union with Christ as described through the Vine and the branch relationship in John 15.

We thought that the Lord wanted us to use our gifts and training to present lessons in discipleship. We planned to use multi-image slides as the medium and draw lessons from nature to teach spiritual truths, even as Jesus did through His use of parables in the New Testament.

Sometimes the Lord gives us just a glimpse of His plan to get us moving in the right direction. Then, as we take further steps of obedience, we see that His plan is a little different from what we first thought. For us, we found that the plan He was about to unfold was more amazing than anything we could ever have imagined.

During Alline's time of service in the Philippines, I lived in my mother's home in Iowa, holding a job in a local newspaper. One day while I was in prayer, the Lord impressed upon me that I should ask Him for $100,000 for our future ministry. I had no idea why we needed all that money, but I began to pray for $100,000!

Alline returned to the U.S. in the summer of 1977. I had moved to Atlanta before her arrival and had settled into a temporary apartment. Alline moved in with me. We knew that the Lord would have to provide a place for us to live and carry on our ministry. An apartment would be too small, for we needed an office for our work plus three bedrooms—one for each of us and a guest room. So, although we had no furniture and no money in savings, we asked the Lord for a three-bedroom *house!* Alline added a request on the side, saying, "Lord, please make it centrally located so that our friends coming into Atlanta will not have a hard time finding us!" It was a bold request, but we had seen the Lord do many wonderful things in answer to prayer. We had been walking this kind of faith life for years at the mission. So we put our trust in the great El-Shaddai, our all-sufficient One. He is the One who said, "Ask and ye shall receive." We also believed the words of Paul in Philippians 4:19, "My God shall supply all your need according to His riches in glory by Christ Jesus." We were taking steps now that looked foolish in the natural, but then, we've discovered that the Lord often calls us to take blind steps of obedience so that He can demonstrate His love and power and raise up a testimony to His greatness.

So—we stepped out of the boat and onto the water.

This, then, is the story of two weak women and God's amazing grace.

Alline Marshall and Bonnie Hanson

2

The Astonishing Answer

About a week after we had prayed for a three-bedroom house, a lady I had never met before came up to me in the corridor of our church.

She said, "Do you ladies have a place to stay yet?"

"No," I replied.

"I think I know of a place where you can stay, but I will need to make a phone call first. I will call you tomorrow," she said.

During the few weeks since Alline had returned from the Philippines, she had fallen down a flight of stairs in a friend's house and had broken her leg. So she was out of action and lying around with a cast on her leg.

The next day the phone rang. It was the lady calling again.

"Would you like to come and see this place?" she asked. "It is a three-story, brick townhouse."

When Alline heard the word *townhouse* she was off the bed in a hurry, onto her crutches, and hurrying to the car. We drove up Peachtree Street to the address the lady had given us. We were driving a very "tired" old 1964 Buick which Alline had purchased while she was teaching college. The neighborhood in which we found ourselves was *posh*. We parked our old car in front of a mansion and walked across the street to the townhouse. It was one of four brick townhouses on that street. There was a fifth one on the corner, separate from the others. The resident in the corner home was the chief anaesthesiologist from Crawford Long Hospital. On one side of our townhouse lived a doctor from Piedmont Hospital. On the other side, a dentist and a civil engineer resided. We two "church mice" followed the lady up the curving steps that were graced with a wrought-iron rail covered with trailing ivy. She unlocked the front door and told us to step inside. We did—onto a beautiful oriental rug! At our left was a lovely circular stairway leading to the upstairs. To the right through a wide doorway was a formal dining room with a huge, sparkling, crystal chandelier hanging over a polished dining table circled with elegant chairs. These were all sitting on another beautiful oriental rug. Other fine pieces of furniture graced the walls.

I walked down the hall past the half bath and well-equipped kitchen to the spacious living room. This room, which covered the entire width of the house, had a fireplace at one end. The whole room was furnished with elegance and style. Double French doors led out onto a private walled-in patio. A double garage extended from the rear wall of the patio. Upstairs, the master bedroom, again the width of the house in size, was furnished beautifully with a four-poster, queen-sized bed and several fine pieces of furniture. This room also included a nice fireplace. There was another comfortable bedroom furnished in maple. There were two full baths and spacious closets. Downstairs, below the main floor, was another bedroom the width of the house with a private bath. The Lord had given us our three-bedroom house all right, and completely furnished, too! It was a woman's dream!!

Because of her broken leg, Alline was not able to tour the house. But she said later that she didn't really need to see the rest of the house to know that she wouldn't find it hard to live there!

When I returned to the front hall where Alline and the lady were chatting, the friend placed the key to the house in my hand and said, "The rent will be to pray for our unsaved loved ones." We were astonished, to say the least! And we were more than happy to pay that rent. I really didn't sleep much that night because of my excitement. I couldn't *imagine* the Lord giving us such a *castle* in which to begin our new work! We moved in immediately. For months I felt like a visitor, waiting for the lady of the house to come home. I had never lived in such elegance.

We had a ball! We hosted missionary guests and held meetings with speakers. We believe that many of our guests were encouraged in their faith when they saw what the Lord had done for us in answer to prayer.

Oh yes, and what about the second part of our original prayer for a house that would be centrally located? This house was just one block off Peachtree Street, half way between Buckhead and downtown Atlanta. It was only four blocks from the Amtrack station and four blocks from the junction of I–75 and I–85 at Peachtree. We could scarcely have been more central.

One day, the owner of the house contacted us and regretfully said that she had discovered that the IRS would not allow her to give out rental property on a free basis. So she had to charge us a minimal rent. Even though the rent was small, it was a stretch of faith for us. But the Lord met it, and we went forward, trying to prepare for our new ministry.

Then the owner contacted us again and said that she wanted to do something for our work—as though she hadn't already! So she began to pay for our utilities—heat, electricity, water—everything but the phone bill. It was a wonderful provision for us!

We loved to have a fire in our townhouse fireplace in the evenings, but where could we find firewood in the heart of the city? The Lord knew. One day a crew of men came down the street cutting limbs from the trees and even taking some trees down. We went out and asked if we could have some firewood. Not only did they cut up a pile of wood, they delivered it to our garage, and we had a supply for many nice evening fires. **The Lord's ways are so unique.**

Two Weak Women

To prepare for our multi-image slide ministry, we traveled to Indiana to the studio of Christian film producer, Ken Anderson. He presents seminars to help missionaries upgrade their film and slide presentations. There we learned much about slide equipment and techniques.

We were also involved in Christian-book distribution in the Savannah, Georgia area. A friend asked us to service a set of book racks in gift shops, 7–11 stores, and grocery stores. So every month or six weeks we loaded the old Buick with books and set off to the coast to spread the Word through good books. We praise the Lord for the books that touched lives through this outreach.

There had been no time limit set on our stay at the townhouse. We had lived there for about eighteen months when the Lord suddenly changed our entire course again!

3

A Life-Changing Dream

God moves in a mysterious way, His wonders to perform." Thus reads the well-loved hymn, and in our case, God certainly did move in both mysterious and wonderful ways.

One July night during the second summer we lived in the townhouse, I had a dream. It was such a vivid dream and played out in such detail that it was still with me strongly when I awoke. It was so clear that it was as if I had seen a television program the night before. When I went downstairs for breakfast the next morning, I told Alline about it.

"I dreamed that the Lord has given us a fifty-five acre property!"

"Well!" she exclaimed. "Thank you, Lord, for fifty-five acres!"

That may have been unknowingly her first statement of faith about the property. During the next few days, I had a sense that the fulfillment was imminent. By Friday morning I felt that we should ask the Lord to show us *that day* where the property was located! We didn't know whether He wanted us to go out looking for land, or whether He planned to "drop it into our laps" as He had the townhouse. So we prayed that He would show us. But nothing happened. No one came, no one called.

That evening Alline planned to attend the ordination service of our youth pastor. I decided that I should go with her, since this would be the last opportunity *that* day for someone to say something to us about the property. We sat down in the pew, and Alline picked up the special bulletin which had been prepared for the service. In it was a listing of pastors who were to ordain the young man. One was listed but not present. This was Rev. Ralph Godwin, who happened to be the Christian and Missionary Alliance pastor in Albany, Georgia, Alline's hometown. When she saw his name she whispered to me, "Someday when I am home again, I would like to visit this man's church." We didn't realize it that night, but this was the Lord putting His finger on the name of the man who would be the link to the fifty-five acres! And He did it *that very day!*

As it happened, Alline had an errand to do in Albany that weekend. So on Sunday she attended Rev. Godwin's church. Afterward, she chatted with him about the work we were planning to begin. He became so interested that he called Alline that afternoon to discuss our vision some more. As they talked, Alline mentioned that she believed the Lord was going to place us in a retreat location someday.

"Well," said Rev. Godwin, "I don't know if this would be of interest to you, but I used to be on the board at Toccoa Falls College, and I know that the Child Evangelism Fellowship is trying to sell their children's camp north of Toccoa."

Alline returned to Atlanta on Tuesday with that news. I was so *excited!* Maybe this was *it!* I eagerly called the offices of Child Evangelism Fellowship (C.E.F.) in Atlanta.

"Yes, it is for sale," the lady said, "but we don't have the details here."

She gave me the name and number of the man in Toccoa (in the mountains of northeast Georgia) who was handling it for them. That night we called him long distance to get more details. I cocked the phone between my shoulder and ear, listening as he gave me the information and writing it down on a piece of paper in my hand.

"It has ten buildings and two little lakes," he was saying.

Alline was sitting next to me and was about to nudge me with her elbow to ask him, "How many acres?" She was thinking of the dream I had.

Before she could do that, he said to me, "And it has *fifty-five acres!*"

I nearly fell over! Then I bravely asked, "How much are they asking for it?" This was such a ridiculous question. Here we were, two virtually penniless, missionary ladies barely meeting our rent and living expenses, and we are asking about a *fifty-five acre property* in the north Georgia mountains?

He said, "Well, they have been talking about $110,000, but I'm sure they are going to sell it for $100,000."

With that I nearly *did* fall over. I had been praying for over eighteen months for $100,000 as the Lord had directed me back in Iowa. Alline had joined me in that prayer when she returned from the Philippines. This was *it*, no doubt about it! I didn't sleep much that night either!

The next morning we drove up to the mountains to see the realtor, John Hood, about the property. We sat with him and his wife in their living room, sharing about ourselves and what we planned to do. He must have thought he was dealing with some rather strange people. Here were two missionaries with no money wanting to look at a $100,000 property! But we discovered that he was a man of faith, too. He said he would rather deal with us than with a millionaire, for he *knew* the *Lord* had the money! So he took us seventeen miles out into the boondocks to see the land. It was a beautiful, remote valley surrounded by heavy forest. The fifty-five acres were located in the foothills of the Blue Ridge Mountains in northeast Georgia. It was and still is a choice area, only one hundred miles from Atlanta. Its easy accessibility to various metropolitan areas in the southeast have made it highly desirable to many groups who need a place of quietness where they can meet with the Lord. We will never forget that first day when we followed John Hood up that mile of graveled road and took our initial look at the property. The grounds and buildings were very run down and unkempt. The camp had lain dormant for several years with only a resident couple living as a presence in the main house. Little or no maintenance had been done. But the Lord blinded our eyes to the condition of the land and facilities. What we saw was the POTENTIAL. And that continues to be the key word—POTENTIAL. We have not yet reached our potential, but we are working hard in that direction.

Mr. Hood walked around with us to see some of the buildings and then left us on our own to roam as we pleased. Alline and I went back into the forest behind the buildings, and by the time we had gone about one hundred yards into the woods, we couldn't see any of the buildings at all. We suddenly realized that we were lost! Undaunted, we climbed a mountain behind the retreat. Alline is adventuresome, and she had urged me to climb the mountain with her. By the time we had reached the top, I could scarcely speak. Heart patients should never attempt such a climb, I discovered. As we came down the mountain, we noticed that the sun was going down, and we still didn't know where we were. But finally, we found an old forestry road and made our way out to the graveled county road to safety.

We were elated and excited. We *knew* that we had found the property the Lord had spoken to us about. As we rode back down I–85 to Atlanta that evening, we were already talking about what we should name the property! There was no question but that we would take it on. (In the months that followed, we decided to keep the name C.E.F. had used—Fellowship Valley). Alline said to me as we rode home that night, "Did you notice that the Lord has that place *monogrammed* for us?" On the peaks of three of the buildings were white, wooden letters about fifteen inches high—FV. Of course, they really stood for Fellowship Valley, but it thrilled us to think of it in terms of our own corporate ministry name—*Faith Ventures.*

The reality that we now faced was this: It is one thing to see an exhilarating vision of what God wants to do. It is quite

The main house, as it was the first day we stood on the property.

The main house, as it is today.

One of the cabins.

The old mill with water wheel

Our main lake.

Alline, hiking into the forest the first day we saw the retreat.

A youth retreat in 1996.

another thing to see the funds and supplies come in to bring it into the visible. I realized too, that it is one thing to be part of a mission ministry where the responsibility to trust the Lord for great needs is spread out among a *number* of people. It is *another* kind of adventure for two lone women to launch out on their own. We were about to learn in a much larger way what His Word means when it says, "Now *faith is the substance of things hoped for, the evidence of things not seen*" (Hebrews 11:1).

4

Like the Eagles

Now we were *soaring*, launched on an adventure we could never fully describe to anyone else. The Lord was taking us up into a realm we had not seen before, a place of "rarified air."

Penniless, yes. We were still without money. In the natural it was almost ridiculous. But we had discovered that when the *Lord* takes us up for some purpose of His own, there is no need for concern about how it is going to happen. It is simply GOING TO HAPPEN!

The next weekend, Alline attended a church service on Sunday night in Valdosta, Georgia. Before the service a friend introduced to her, Tom Gregory, a fine architect. During the service Alline was asked to give a testimony. She stood up and described what was happening in our work and told about the dream and the property. Afterward, Tom came up to her and said, "I happen to have some business in Toccoa next Thursday. If you ladies would like to be up at your place, I will be glad to come and give you some ideas about it."

So here we were! We hadn't put a penny down on the property yet, but the Lord had already given us an *architect*! Never mind, it is perfectly safe to follow on when the LORD is leading, for the Lord works in unorthodox ways. He is fully able to fill in that great void where there are no funds. So, naturally, we were at the property that Thursday. We walked around with Tom, took pictures of "our place" and talked. We were sitting near the campfire circle on the lake shore enjoying a picnic lunch together when we saw two strangers walking along the shoreline. It was another realtor showing someone else OUR PLACE!! It was a shock for us to realize that someone else was interested in the property. We came to learn that it had lain dormant on the market for several years, and then, more recently, it had been listed in a national magazine. Now there were people from far and wide coming to look at it. We went home that day *determined* to scrape together everything we had to put a $1,000 option on the land to hold it. But when we scraped, we found that we didn't *have* $1,000! There was nothing we could do except pray and trust the Lord to hold it until such a time as He chose to provide the money.

It was late August of 1978 when we had walked the land with our architect. When Labor Day weekend came, we received an urgent call from our realtor.

"Can't you *possibly* get an option payment down on the place?" he urged. "There is an interested couple coming up this weekend from Florida, and they may take it."

There was still nothing we could do except to trust the Lord. And He held it for us.

The weeks flew by, and we found ourselves with a real timing crunch in early October. We were expecting two long-term guests. Looking after them would tie us down for some weeks, and we were very concerned that a prospective buyer might come along and take the property while we were busy with guests. We needed to drive to Missouri to negotiate with the owners of Fellowship Valley before our guests came, but we had no option money to offer them.

It was the first week of October, and it was also Wednesday, the morning for our women's missionary prayer meeting at church. Alline was just going out the door when the phone rang. I picked it up. It was the architect calling. Alline went on to the meeting, and I sat down to talk with him. He wanted some information about the buildings at the retreat. Then he asked me how the finances were coming. I didn't have much to report except that we really needed to see the Lord meet us so that we could go to Missouri to negotiate for the land before our guests arrived. We hung up. About thirty minutes later the phone rang again. It was the architect on the line once more.

"You ladies go ahead and do your negotiating," he said, "The check for your option money will be in the mail Monday."

What an exciting moment! The next morning we were on our way, picnic basket in hand and our realtor in tow!

You really needed to be a mouse in the corner to appreciate the scene as we sat down in the office of the president of Child Evangelism Fellowship. We were utterly naive in matters of real estate. I had never purchased anything larger than a dishpan in my life. Alline, at least, had bought a car, but that hardly compared to purchasing property for $100,000! We chatted with the Child Evangelism Fellowship men for awhile, and then they took us out to dinner at a nice restaurant. As we sat visiting and sharing, the president turned to Alline and said, "You DO have the down payment, don't you?"

"Why *no!*" exclaimed a surprised Alline. Fact was, we didn't even have the option check in hand to give to him. That was still on its way to us in the mail.

The C.E.F. president was shocked and silent for a moment. Then he said, "Well, I believe that I have just as much faith in God as *you* do."

And with that, he allowed us to sign the contract without paying any money down and without his ever having seen us before!

We started back to Atlanta with our realtor. As we rode along he said to us, " You know, this was going to be the final property sale for my wife and me before we go into full-time Christian service. We have been praying about this, and we believe that the Lord would have us tithe our commission on this sale back to *you* folks!"

So through those first years, when *we* made a payment on Fellowship Valley, we received a check from the *realtor!* Over the years we received most of our option money back again. The Lord has wonderful ways of handling real estate—townhouses and mountain property alike!

These were the first small steps in our new faith walk, but they were part of the fulfillment of His promise, "Faith is the substance of things hoped for, the evidence of things not seen" (Hebrews 11:1). And they strengthened us for the larger steps just ahead.

5

The Big Leap

Lord, you've got us out on a limb. Now saw it off and let us fall into the everlasting arms," prayed a missionary candidate during a great financial crisis.

That prayer certainly suited our situation when we closed on the contract for the fifty-five acres called Fellowship Valley. When we signed our names, the Lord sawed off the limb behind us. One thing certainly impresses me as I recount this adventure: There was no *fear*. Taking the awesome step of signing a paper which committed us to pay off a debt of $147,000 (including interest) in ten years held no fear for us! It was breathtaking, but it was as though we were moving in a sphere where we didn't have normal, human reactions. We had been swept up into a commitment that was God's responsibility to fulfill, not ours. He had begun the venture in amazing ways, and He would *complete* it in just such a manner. We were walking this commitment with God, but *He* was actually *doing* the work of it.

We had only one Source to whom we could look for the funds. We believed God's Word, that He would supply all our needs. So trusting Him to provide became our strategy as we began the three-month option period Child Evangelism Fellowship had given us. We needed $9,000 to complete the down payment. We knew that it would take a miracle to obtain this amount of money before the deadline. We were two lone women, but we had many praying friends who represented the *visible* forces. In, beyond, and surrounding all of this was El-Shaddai, the invisible, all-sufficient One.

As the Apostle James teaches, we put works together with our faith and began attending garage and estate sales. The buildings at Fellowship Valley were nearly bereft of furnishings. We also had five kitchens to equip. We began acquiring rugs, a washer and dryer, chairs, and other needed items. Half of our double garage was quickly filling up with our garage-sale "treasures." We never dared to have our garage door up when our doctor neighbor passed by in his white Porsche on the way to his garage. Ours looked like a used furniture store; his looked like an operating room with everything neatly in place.

My mother helped us by upholstering some of the well-worn furniture we brought home. She worked in the garage under real hardship, for we didn't have a sewing machine for her to use. But just at that time, a friend gave us a fine, portable Singer machine. Praise the Lord!

By early November our collection of goods had piled toward the roof and overflowed the space. So we decided to borrow a moving truck and take our goods up to the retreat property. We didn't have the down payment yet, but that didn't matter. We *knew* this was the place God had indicated! It was ours by faith! We found two men to load the truck and drive it up to the mountains for us. Once there, we unloaded it in one end of the dining room where the roof didn't leak—to await our ultimate arrival!

During those weeks the Lord allowed some lovely things to happen to encourage us and to assure us that He was really with us in this great adventure. A man approached us at church one Sunday and said, "You're going to need a lot of *paint* up there, aren't you?" We agreed, and he said, "I think we can help you." He returned in a short time with a gift of 150 gallons of interior and exterior paint!

The Big Leap

Another man from our church came to the townhouse one evening to pick up our missionary guest. As they were leaving the house, our friend from the church turned to me and said, "You will need a lot of beds up there, won't you?"

"Yes," I replied, rather surprised that someone would ask about such a big item as beds.

"How many do you need?" he persisted.

"Well, I guess about a hundred!" I quickly "guesstimated."

"I think we can help you with that," he said as he turned to leave.

I stood there amazed. We later learned that he was the head of a foundation for a motel chain. Every few years motels find it necessary to replace their beds. By law they cannot sell the used beds, so they give them away. This gentleman had *thousands* of beds to give away just then. The problem was that we could not use very many *double* beds. We needed mostly twins. We did receive three double beds from him, and he also gave us eighteen lamps, about twenty-five lounge chairs, three dinette sets, and a number of two-drawer dressers. It was a wonderful provision for our barren buildings.

We began to run back and forth to the mountains frequently to consult with the people at the county courthouse in Clarkesville about the property and with the man at the health department about the well. Alline's car was a gas guzzler, so she said, "Let's pray for a small car that won't use so much gas." So we prayed.

About a week later a couple came up to us at church and asked, "Could you use a car? We have a Karman Ghia we would like to give to you."

We didn't even know what a Karman Ghia *was!* But we soon found out that it was a sports car of the Volkswagen family. So now we had our small car! Alline said that the Lord had a good sense of humor giving two missionary spinsters a *sports* car!

One morning before dawn the phone rang. I picked it up and sat in the dark listening as a man calling from up in the mountains said, "I understand that you ladies are buying Fellowship Valley. I am interested in that property. I have had masonry and carpentry training, and I am wondering if the Lord would have me be your maintenance man."

There was nothing that these two women needed more than a *maintenance* man in *that* awful mess. He did come along and help us for awhile when we moved to the retreat. Our hearts were really lifted and excited by these unusual moves of the Lord in our behalf!

The challenge of raising nine thousand dollars for the down payment continued to test our faith as only small gifts of money trickled in. As we neared and finally came to the December deadline, we were dismayed. We didn't have *nearly* enough money for the payment. We *knew* that God was *in* this faith step. He had sealed it in many ways. But where was the *money?* I confess I sank into a momentary "hole." We decided that there was no alternative but to ask C.E.F. for an extension on the option period. Meanwhile, we were aware that there was a couple from New Jersey waiting with a contract on Fellowship Valley written with another realtor. They had cash in hand and were ready to take the property if we forfeited. C.E.F. graciously gave us a two-month extension. We prayed and others prayed with us and the gifts continued to come in. By mid-February we needed about $3,000, and then it was down to $1200. When we came to the last day of February—the deadline—we still needed $469 to complete the payment. It might as well have been $4,000! We didn't have it, and we didn't know where we could get it.

Alline announced, "We are going to have a *praise party!* The Lord is going to send in that money!"

So, off we went to the scheduled women's missionary prayer fellowship at church. The ladies prayed for us and for our need, then we divided into small groups to pray for foreign missions' needs. Afterward, on our way back to the main meeting room, a lady approached Alline and pressed a folded piece of paper into her hand. When Alline opened the paper, it was a check for $469!! It was the exact amount needed to finish the payment! What an exciting moment! When we entered the meeting room, there we saw a party table spread with punch and goodies! Actually, the ladies were celebrating the eightieth birthdays of two of their members. But when we told them how the Lord had just met our need, we all sang the Doxology, and we had our praise party, complete with punch and goodies!

We were now launched! We began to pack our belongings in earnest for the move to the mountains. We looked like old-time "Okies" as we piled our car full and drove to the retreat again and again. Then, with the use of a borrowed van, we finally completed our move. New friends in the mountains helped us unload and settle in with our goods. We were now officially mountaineers, or hillbillies, and we were *excited!*

6

The University of "Hard Knocks"

Nothing could ever have prepared two city girls for the mysteries and idiosyncrasies of septic tanks, drain fields, pumphouses, and tainted well water.

Our practical education began about two weeks before we moved in. The young couple C.E.F. had installed in the main house to "baby-sit" the property were now moving on to a ministry in Texas. They put their small car into a large moving van and then brought the truck to the retreat to load the rest of their goods. They backed the truck up to the kitchen steps of the house, at least they *tried* to! The moment the rear wheels of that heavily-laden truck rolled onto the cement slab near the steps, they discovered where the *septic tank* was!! The double rear wheels crashed through the lid, dropping the concrete pieces to the bottom of the tank. A tow truck had to be called to lift the truck out of the hole. What a mess!! Well, at least that was *one* tank we didn't have to search for in the months ahead.

The mystery of where the septic tank was located for each building became an important part of our introduction to country living. No, we didn't go looking for them every day. Usually, the search began when we had a dread emergency—a sewage backup. *Then* we had a crisis on hand and *had* to find the exact location of the tank in question. It took a lot of searching, prodding into the earth with steel rods, and just plain digging here and there to discover the tanks finally!

We were sitting in one of the lakeside cabins one afternoon having tea with two ladies from Gainesville. Suddenly, we heard the strange sound of gurgling water coming from the bathroom. It was *running* all right—over the rim of the stool and all over the new rug. And it was flowing right on into the living room, soaking that rug with the kind of brackish waters no one likes to *think* about at a tea party! Bedlam followed as I rushed off to obtain a plumbing tool we didn't have. Meanwhile, our two guests helped Alline drag all the furniture out of the living room and put it outside on the grass.

Oh, yes, we learned some great lessons about plumbing mysteries that day. Apparently, the three cabins were all hooked in sequence on the same sewage line. The first cabin up the row had suddenly developed problems, and this set off the eruption in our bathroom in the last cabin on the line. We always marveled, too, that the sewage pipe, rather than going directly into the septic tank, made no less than four ninety-degree turns behind that cabin before making its entrance into the tank. We also came to understand the problem of tree roots clogging the drain lines and stopping the works.

The puzzling layout of our water lines, in addition to their relation to the well, was another challenge. We had learned at the health department before we moved in that our well needed to be purged to clear it of bacteria. We scratched our heads over this, wondering why the couple who had lived on the place had never looked into this. Nevertheless, we two novices, together with the dauntless head of the health department, began the task of searching for the lines and then cleansing the well. We went to the little pump house, and from that point we were confounded by a set of pipes which seemed to be trailing off in strange directions. There were two pumps and two holding tanks in the pump house. After studying the maze of pipes, the health department agent began to wonder whether we might be pumping our water directly from the *lake!!* (We were not!)

The mystery of the water lines was not solved that day, but we decided to go on with the purging of the well. Following our friend's good instructions, we proceeded to pour a large quantity of Chlorox into the hole at the top of the well. We waited the specified time and then turned on the faucets in our home, confident that we would smell the chlorine. The odor would signal that the lines were clean. Well, we ran the water and ran the water, but no chlorine odor *ever* came through. So we went back to our friend at the health department. He gave us some *industrial strength* chlorine tablets. We dutifully dropped those into the well and waited, and then turned on the faucets. Nothing! There was no indication at all that we had accomplished the job. Obviously, we had a "different" kind of well. We have concluded in the years since that we have so much water from adjacent springs flowing through this bored well that the chlorine washes away before it can come through the lines. What else can explain it? We are happily amazed at this thirty-four-foot bored well that has never gone dry even during drought years. It serves up water to our home, four cabins, a dormitory (which holds twenty people), and the main kitchen building. It is a fine well with good water, and we thank the Lord for this blessing.

The *water lines* were a different story. We have managed to find most of them by trial or error over the years. But again, the surest way to discover where the lines were was to have a large group due in a few hours. Then, inevitably, an underground line would pop open, and suddenly we had a new bubbling spring on the grounds. Our local plumber was very kind in rushing to our rescue in such emergencies. At other times, Alline had swung into action and delivered us from our dilemma!

Many of the old buildings at Fellowship Valley were built for a children's summer camp, so they were not winterized. Pipes needed to be insulated under the cabins as well as inside the cabins. I don't know how many times I went to the bunkroom in the winter and found a geyser of water shooting toward the ceiling from a broken water line and a flood of water covering the floor.

We also saw the ravages of floor and wall rot because the buildings had been built too close to the ground. When we first arrived at Fellowship Valley, the toilet in cabin three was leaning at a forty-five-degree angle, propped up by a two-by-four. The floor board had to be replaced around it. A dresser fell right through the floor in that same cabin! We learned so many things through the years that Alline said: "If the Lord should ever take us out of retreat work, we could go into development!"

Our education continues.

7

Joy at the Midnight Hour

There is no way to describe our new "walk on the water." We had signed our names to a contract for $100,000 without so much as a dollar having been exchanged between us and Child Evangelism Fellowship. It had been seemingly such a simple transaction, almost like buying a car. But now we were committed to a mortgage of $147,000, including the interest. Yet, there was no shadow of fear lurking around our hearts. We were caught up in an amazing venture, and the only way through the obstacles was by moving ahead and keeping our eyes on the Lord!

The contract stated that we would meet an annual payment of about $14,600 at the end of February for ten years. This was a staggering amount for two lone women to meet. Humanly speaking, it seems easier to trust the Lord to meet large needs when we are regularly fellowshipping with close friends and prayer partners who stand with us in faith for the need. So when we moved to our isolated valley in the mountains, we were launched on a new solitary walk with God, which we had never experienced before. We had no big, financial backers; no churches underwriting this property venture. It was two weak women and the Lord—El-Shaddai, "the more than enough God."

We had many expenses to meet on a daily basis to pay for

the utilities, buy lumber and plumbing supplies, and do remodeling. So the gifts that came in during the early part of the year had to be used for general expenses. They could not be saved toward the payment due in February of the next year. The breathtaking phenomenon was that the Lord never seemed to begin sending gifts toward the property payment until late November or early December. That gave us about three months to see this enormous amount come in. The Lord seems to delight in allowing His servants to walk through a testing period to exercise their trust in Him. He often brings us to the midnight hour of our need and then reveals His wonderful answer. This is what we witnessed year after year. We admit that in some of the later years we went beyond the midnight hour, but nevertheless, He always met the need in good time.

The first year that we were living at the retreat, we came to Monday of the last week of February, and we still needed $6,700 to complete the payment. We didn't know where it would come from, but Alline said, "We are just going to praise the Lord! He is going to send the money!" The next morning the telephone rang. It was a gentleman calling from the far west.

"We are sending you a gift of $5,000," he said.

"Praise the Lord!" exclaimed Alline.

"How much more do you need for your payment this year?" asked the caller.

"Seventeen hundred by Saturday," replied Alline rather timidly.

"Well, I think your benefactor can cover that all right," he said. "I'll just send you a check for the whole amount."

And he did! Praise the Lord for His faithfulness!

In November of 1986, we received a letter from a man in Atlanta who had never been a donor before. It was the Thanksgiving holiday, and his short note with the check simply said, "As I count my blessings." The check was for $10,000! Then came *another* check from the same gentleman. There wasn't

Joy at the Midnight Hour

even a *note* enclosed this time, and again the check was for $10,000! What a special blessing these were, for we also had a great need for additional funds to buy lumber and other supplies for work projects for the next month. These gifts met both needs, and we rejoiced.

Gifts for the property payment came in unusual ways and in differing amounts. Some were as small as five dollars from a retired couple living on a limited income.

One friend wrote that she had a dream one night. In the dream she saw Alline in our Fellowship Valley kitchen, and she was quite concerned about the annual payment need. When the friend awoke the next morning, she asked the Lord if He wanted to say something to her through this dream. "Send them $1,000," came His reply. She told her husband about the dream, and he nearly had a *stroke!* One thousand dollars was no small amount for this struggling family. Nevertheless, in obedience to God, the husband prayed about the matter. It took him three weeks to find the Lord's mind on it, but confirm it He did. Their letter contained a check for $1,000.

In 1989 we came to the last day of February and still needed $7700 of the payment amount. This was for the *final* payment on Fellowship Valley. Once again, we had no idea where the money would come from. Midmorning that day the telephone rang. It was a young man calling from Atlanta. We had just met him and his wife about three weeks earlier, and they had expressed great interest in the work. In fact his reason for calling now was to ask when they could come for a week as volunteer workers. As he continued visiting with Alline on the phone, he asked her if this was the time the annual payment was due.

"Yes," replied Alline, "It is today."

"How are the funds coming along?" he asked.

"Well, we are moving in the right direction but we aren't there yet."

"How much do you need," he persisted.

"Seven thousand," she responded. (We were able to care for the $700).

"I would like to write you a check for that amount," he said. And he did! He drove up from Atlanta to deliver it to us the next day. What a wonderful climax to the many years of making payments on the retreat! What a deliverance!

We were so relieved to step out free from the responsibility of this mortgage. We marvel when we consider that the Lord sent in not only the $147,000 for the property, but many additional thousands of dollars for the upgrading of the grounds and buildings. The financial miracle was, and continues to be, a very big one! All glory to Him.

All of the faith lessons and experiences we encountered in those years were merely the preparation for GREATER things which only the Lord knew about. When we first launched out we would probably have been afraid had we known all that the future held in the way of faith challenges. God has brought us along so graciously and taught us to trust Him more deeply as we have walked in His way.

When we first saw the property, we didn't *see* the innumerable problems related to repairing and resurrecting it. The Lord allowed us to see only the *potential* of it. And we have not achieved our potential *yet!!* However, with the mortgage out of the way, we were ready for the next great phase of development. Our prayers for supply enlarged as we began to realize the magnitude of the need. Looking back, the initial $100,000 seems like a very small amount indeed. The amount we need now is in the range of several million. WE NEED TO BUILD!

The first encouragement we received toward the new buildings was a gift of two dollars from a widow in Pennsylvania. Then came a gift of one hundred dollars from one of the ladies in a group of military wives who came to Fellowship Valley on retreat.

Are you asking the question the disciples asked, "Lord, what is this among so many?" We have the same Lord who took five loaves and two fishes and multiplied them so there was enough to feed five thousand people. "With God, all things are possible!!" We are now waiting before Him for the full amount with which to build urgently needed buildings.

8

Amazing Grace!

We need a truck!! That realization came very soon after we arrived in the mountains. We faced a mammoth cleanup of the grounds. So we began to ask around in our church in Atlanta to see if anyone had a pickup truck we could buy reasonably.

We found a man who had a 1965 GMC truck. It was a six-cylinder, stick-shift model, rusty and dented. No one knew how many miles it had on its odometer, but it still ran! That was the important thing. We bought it for "a song" and brought it to the mountains. We hand-painted it bright blue, trimmed it in white, and named it, "Amazing Grace." Alline said that it was amazing it still ran.

The two of us began to load the truck frequently with the junk and cast-off goods we found around the retreat and took the trash to the county landfill. There were some jobs too big for us to tackle, like the pile of nearly two dozen cotton mattresses stacked in a lakeside cabin under a leaky roof! What a stench!

Trips to the landfill became part of our regular schedule. One morning we piled the truck very high with trash, then threw an old, double bedspring on top of the load. We left the grounds from our back gate and started up the narrow, winding gravel road toward the ridge. Our retreat is down in a private valley, surrounded by heavily forested hills and a mountain, so we have to go up a steep, narrow, winding, graveled road to get out to the paved highway. Alline was driving, and she failed to get up enough speed in the old truck to carry us all the way up the hill to the ridge. The engine began to sputter, cough, hesitate, and then it suddenly died!! We began to roll backward down the hill with this huge load of junk. Alline jumped on the brakes, but she discovered to her horror that there *were* no brakes!!

We were careening faster and faster downhill at a wild rate. Looking in the outside rearview mirror, Alline was frantically trying to steer the truck safely backward and keep us on the road. I was really frightened!! I began to cry out loudly to the Lord for help! My heart was stuck somewhere up in my throat! Suddenly, the thought flashed into my mind—-the *hand* brake!! "Try the hand brake!" I shouted to Alline. She did, and finally she brought us to a halt without a disaster. *I* was ready to go *home!* I was very shaken. But not Alline. She cranked up the old engine and away we went right back up the hill again. She didn't even know whether or not we had *brakes*. We found out later that the problem was a leaky brake cylinder. We had brakes when going forward, but not when going backward!

As we drove along the highway toward town with our load, I was still praying, but I was praying silently now. I had had enough of that truck. This was the second serious incident we had experienced with it. "PLEASE, Lord, give us a new truck," I pleaded fervently.

The next morning the telephone rang. It was a woman calling from Toccoa. She said to me, "How is your old pickup truck doing? Could you use another one? I have one over here that I would like to give to you." We were elated! Then she said, "How about a *dump* truck? Could you use that, too?" We thought that over and decided to accept it. We must have been thinking of all the stuff we could carry away in a *big* truck. Then she asked, "How about a front-end loader? Could you use that, too?" We were astonished but grateful, and we received all of the equipment. Her husband had recently suffered a heart attack and gone home to be with the Lord. His equipment was sitting in her backyard and she wanted it to be used in the Lord's work. I had never had a quicker answer to prayer in my life, except for my salvation.

The front grill on our first pickup truck, "Amazing Grace," had the large metal letters GMC on it. Alline said that this meant GRACE, MORE COMING! So when the second truck arrived, we named it "More Grace!"

I believe the Lord sent a troop of angels out with Alline each time she drove those old trucks. Something always seemed to happen to her and the trucks! I began to have a real concern for her very life when she continued having these incidents. Given the ancient vintage of the trucks, I wondered what would happen if something even as small as a tie rod should break.

One day Alline and our maintenance helper, Mike, were returning home with a heavy load of lumber that had been given to us. As they came around a curve on highway 441, one of the rear wheels suddenly flew off the truck and sailed off into a nearby field! Alline and Mike careened along on three wheels and an axle before finally coming to a safe stop at the edge of the road.

On another occasion, Alline was driving our "More Grace" pickup when she felt that something just wasn't right. So she pulled over onto the shoulder of the road. She had scarcely stopped when a tire exploded with a *bang!*

Another day, she was rushing along down a long hill in "Amazing Grace" when suddenly the *hood* flew up in her face. The only way she could see the highway ahead was through the narrow space between the dashboard and the bottom edge of the hood! As I said before, I am convinced the Lord always sent angels along with Alline whenever she drove those old trucks.

As "More Grace" aged and my concern for Alline's safety increased, we prayed earnestly for a new truck. We prayed for about three years before the wonderful answer came. A friend

The truck named Amazing Grace.

Unloading junk at the landfill.

Alline, the maintenance man!

called us one day and asked, "Could you use a really *good* used truck?"

"Oh *yes*," we exclaimed. She went on to tell us that her son's truck was there. He had been tragically killed in an accident, and the family wanted us to have his truck. We felt so blessed. It was a 1983 heavy-duty, Chevy pickup truck! That updated our truck fleet by nearly twenty years! We were thrilled. We named the truck "Precious Grace," partly because of the cost at which it came to us, and partly because the young man's mother was nicknamed "Precious."

We began to drive this fine truck to town on errands to get lumber and other supplies. We soon found that it drank gas at an alarming rate! So Alline said, "Let's pray for a *small* truck." This would be more economical for running errands in town. We would save the big truck for heavy moving jobs. So we prayed for a small truck. One evening a short time later, the phone rang. It was a gentleman calling from near Macon, Georgia. He said the Lord had awakened him in the night and had spoken to him, saying, "Give those ladies your truck!" He was calling us in obedience to what the Lord had told him to do. As he and Alline chatted, he finally said, "Here's what I'll do. I will give you my truck, but it guzzles gas like yours does. Or, I will sell it and give you the money. Or, I will sell it and buy you a *small* truck!" We chose the small truck! He came to the retreat a short time later to bring us our Mazda truck which we named "Mustard Seed." We were delighted. It has proven to be very useful to us.

We were also in desperate need of a new car. Our old 1964 Buick was showing over 170,000 miles on its odometer. We had been praying about this but never imagined what the Lord had in store for us. A friend called and said that her husband had died and she wanted to give us a gift. We were free to use it as needed. The gift arrived. It was a check for $10,000! We were able to buy a brand-new, mid-size station wagon for the work. It gave us years of wonderful service, and we thank the Lord for His answer to our prayers.

Two Weak Women

In 1995 I was to speak at a missions conference in Pennsylvania. We were driving a Chevy station wagon which had served well, but was now definitely past its prime. In fact we didn't know whether or not it would make the trip safely. Nevertheless, we ventured out on faith and traveled north and completed the first half of the trip without trouble. We had been in Pennsylvania only a few days when we received a call from an old friend in the Pocono Mountains. She asked if we would like to have *her* car! It was a 1993 Oldsmobile with only 39,000 miles on it. What a wonderful answer to our desperate need!! As we traveled south again to Georgia after the conference, we each drove a car. We were moving along well until we were just north of Knoxville, Tennessee. We pulled off at an exit for rest and there the station wagon "died." But isn't the Lord gracious?!! He kept the car going until we had reached the area where our friend and Advisory Board member, Wayne Prosser, lives. Wayne is a mechanic as well as a fine carpenter!! He very kindly drove out to the interstate where we were stranded, purchased a part and installed it on the spot! After a restful, overnight stay with him and his wife in Knoxville, we continued our trip to Georgia. The Lord is merciful.

We have seen and continue to see the Lord provide vehicles of various kinds for us: trucks, a procession of cars, a van, and also some very useful golf carts. When we first came to the Valley, we became *so* tired of walking from one end of the grounds to the other, carrying our tools or whatever we needed for our jobs. Then, through a handicapped young man in Augusta, we received our first golf cart. What a blessing *that* was to our aging legs!! Two other carts came to us from Bethany Fellowship, and others have come in later years to replace old ones. The golf carts and the intercom system have saved more miles on foot than we could ever count! Praise the Lord for those whose thoughtfulness and generosity brought us such gifts.

9

The Baffled Weatherman

We look back with awe on all kinds of miracles even the Lord's control of the weather!

Gifts of foodstuffs began to pour in on us in such a quantity in 1979 that we didn't have room for them in our freezer. So we decided to host a big Thanksgiving-type dinner for all of our friends, including everyone from the little Baptist church we were attending. It was already November, a bit unpredictable for weather, but we bravely, or naively, launched forward. Our dear new friends, Catherine and Royce Porter, volunteered to help. We decided to hold the dinner in the main dining room near the lake. The roof leaked badly, the water lines were cut off for winter, and there was no source of heat in the building as of yet. But nevertheless, we moved ahead.

We set the date, invited some sixty people, and began to prepare. The night before the big dinner, we saw on the weather news that a very big storm system was presently hovering over northwest Georgia. The forecaster promised that this same system would be over northeast Georgia the following day—our BIG day!! We knew that if it rained, everyone at the head table would get wet! (The Ping Pong table served as our main table because we had so few.) We prayed, and we asked others to pray, also. Meanwhile, a friend came and set in a small propane bottle tank and connected it to a small heating stove inside so we would have heat. We carried fresh water over to the main dining room in big kettles. Everything was ready as the morning dawned—gray, but not raining. As the hours went by, and we rushed around preparing food, the weather conditions began to improve. In fact, by the time our guests arrived, the clouds were fluffy white against a beautiful blue sky. It was pleasantly warm outside, and we had a marvelous day! That night, the same weather forecaster showed the big black mass of his previous night's report over northwest Georgia. He was completely baffled and mystified over what had happened to the mass and why it had not gone to northeast Georgia as it should have. HE may have been mystified, but *we* certainly were *not!*

This was just one of many occasions when we saw the Lord change the weather when we prayed. He has been so gracious, giving us many pleasant weekends during which our retreat guests have been able to enjoy their time apart with Him.

Some might say that surely no one can do anything about the *weather!* I only know one Person who can—the same One who stood in a boat with His disciples one stormy night and said to the wind and the waves, "Peace, be still!"

I hasten to say that *sometimes* the Lord chooses to move in other "mysterious ways, His wonders to perform. He plants His footsteps in the sea and rides upon the storm." One weekend He allowed rain to come when we had a group of ladies with us. They were a bit dismayed at first, thinking that it would confine them and keep them from doing the recreational things they had planned. But then on Saturday afternoon, they became involved in a session of sharing and discussion which they themselves would tell you became a *tremendous*, spiritual blessing to them. And that same hymn continues, "His purposes will ripen fast, unfolding every hour. The bud may have a bitter taste, but sweet will be the flower. Ye fearful saints, fresh courage take, the clouds ye so much dread, are big with mercy and shall break with blessing on your head."[1]

---

[1](Wm. Cowper) Light Shining out of Darkness

10

The Blessings of Obedience

One day we took a day trip to Atlanta to see our printer about a job. On our way home that night we stopped briefly to visit with a couple from our church. The husband, Al, asked if we could use an apartment-size electric stove for one of our cabins. We said that we could, so he and his son loaded it into the trunk of our car and we brought it home to the mountains. In those days our driveway went up the hillside from the county road to the top of our lawn. The next day the car was sitting in the yard about twenty-five feet out from our house. The challenge for us was how to get this stove out of the car trunk and into the basement without a handtruck. The three of us (we had a lady helper at this time) managed to wrestle it over the edge of the trunk and slide it to the ground behind the car. There it sat. We didn't know what more to do about it at the moment, so we all went back to our work. Alline was assembling a garden cart, hoping that it would help us boost the stove into the basement. I was upstairs doing housework. I paused long enough to send up a quick SOS to the Lord, saying, "Please, Lord, send us help!"

About thirty minutes later, I heard wheels on the gravel road. It was a red pickup truck, and it rushed down from the mountains behind us, through the valley, and up the ridge at the other side of our retreat. I just took note of it and went back to my work. About a minute later, I heard wheels on gravel again and looked out. I saw the same red pickup truck coming down from the ridge. It turned in at our gate, drove up our driveway, and parked on the lawn right next to the car where the stove was sitting. Out jumped a big, husky, young man! I was so elated at seeing *manpower* arrive, I rushed out onto the little porch outside our kitchen and exclaimed to this total stranger, "Praise the Lord! I just asked the Lord for help, and here you are!"

He looked up at me, and I am sure he was surprised. However, I soon discovered it was no accident that he had stopped. He had been helping at a retreat near Seed Lake that morning and was hurrying home. His wife was waiting lunch for him. As he passed by our gate, the Holy Spirit whispered to him, "*Stop* here and *help* someone." He didn't know us, and he was in a great hurry. But in obedience he turned around and came back to see what the Lord wanted him to do. When he got out of his truck, and I greeted him as I did, he knew he was at the right place. Who would the Lord send to move our electric stove in but an *electrician* from Georgia Power Company! And he was a Christian brother, too! He gladly moved the stove for us and then stayed around for nearly three hours just getting acquainted.

Later, we heard the rest of the story from a pastor. When the young man finally arrived home, his wife was a bit impatient at having to hold lunch so long for him. But he told her what had happened—how he had been passing this place on Bear Gap Road when the Lord told him to stop and help someone. And when he did, these ladies had just asked the Lord for help, and there he was.

Their young son, who was about seven years old, was sitting there taking in this story. The next day he was to attend a birthday party for a friend. When he was all dressed up and had his present wrapped, he got into the car with his mother to go to the party. She put the key into the ignition and tried to start the car, but it would not go. She tried and tried, but the

The Blessings of Obedience

car would not start. She was about to give up when her son said, "No, Mommy, if those ladies can pray and the Lord sends *them* help, we can, too." He bowed his head and prayed. When his mother turned the key again, the car started. If we only had the faith of a child!

11

Help!

Alline and I were hard at work one Spring day during the big cleanup of the early days. Suddenly a van and another vehicle pulled in at our front gate. The doors flew open and a mob of excited, screaming children poured out and ran in every direction. We stood there dumbfounded. The man who was driving one of the cars walked up the front lawn to talk with us. He introduced himself and said that he had worked at Fellowship Valley years ago when it was a children's camp. On this particular day, he was just taking a children's group for a picnic outing and decided to stop and have their outing *here!!* Their visit was totally unannounced and was even more shocking because the retreat was still in such a dire state of disrepair that there were no toilet facilities for groups. In fact, there was no place for a crowd of children even to get a drink of water. Things were still in a rather primitive state. At this point, we hadn't had any workmen in to help us with such projects. After a careful and earnest discussion of our problems, the man loaded up his troop of screaming children and drove away in search of better facilities.

Everywhere we turned there were repair tasks that were beyond our capabilities. Alline, who was our chief maintenance "man," had not yet acquired much knowledge about plumbing, carpentry, and other basic maintenance skills. She had graduated with honors from college, so I teased her that we had the only Phi Beta Kappa maintenance man in north Georgia! To get a "handle" on her lack of knowledge, she bought a library of do-it-yourself books. When the engine on the lawn mower went bad, she studied her book on small engines and then went to work on the mower. She has done very well. She has also become quite adept at using PVC pipe for plumbing when the need arises.

Needless to say, our prayers were urgent when we asked the Lord to send us help!! He answered our prayers in wonderful ways.

We were invited to present a discipleship seminar for adults at an evening Daily Vacation Bible School at a church in South Carolina. Bob and Pauline Johnson were visitors in the class. Bob is a nuclear physicist and later was associated with the "Star Wars" project. He caught the vision of the work in our valley and came to help. He headed a crew to lay a new floor in our main kitchen and helped with other projects on our grounds as well. Bob also presented us with a fine IBM personal computer, which served us well.

Urged by the Lord, volunteer helpers began to flow into the retreat. They fixed gutters, door handles that wouldn't open or shut, repaired plumbing lines, tarred leaky roofs, worked on our ancient trucks, put siding on our house where it had never been completed, fixed rotting floors, painted buildings, remodeled cabins, and labored on a host of other things.

Our car insurance agent, Fred Hamby, was true to his company's slogan: "Like a Good Neighbor, State Farm is There." He came to help plant thirty-six red raspberry bushes which had been given to us, and assisted with other tasks.

A judge and a lawyer kindly offered their counsel free of charge when we needed help with the assessment of our tax exemption papers.

Another skilled helper, Nelson Hower, a former I.R.S. auditor, also counseled us on our tax-exempt papers. After studying our documents he commented that we were the most non-profit, non-profit organization he had ever known.

In those early days workmen came not only to install gift equipment but to help with cleanup. One church in South Carolina sent a large work group to us for two days. Another sent its youth group to do grounds work. Some ladies made curtains and put them up while others helped paint and freshen various rooms.

We had a desperate need for household goods—sheets, blankets, towels, pans, dishes, kitchen utensils, and many other things. The Lord put it into the heart of a dear, retired lady named Alice Farmer to serve as His instrument in this area. Alice and her husband, Al, had operated a secondhand furniture store in Atlanta for years before their retirement to Florida. When they settled into the retirement center, the officials in charge gave them a new responsibility suited to their skills. They were to oversee a room which held the household goods left behind by deceased residents of the home. After receiving permission from the officials, Alice and Al began to pack box after box of dishes, pans, sheets, blankets, silverware,

Alline, practicing her plumbing skills.

Bonnie and Violet, wrapping pipes for winter.

Catherine Porter, painting the main kitchen.

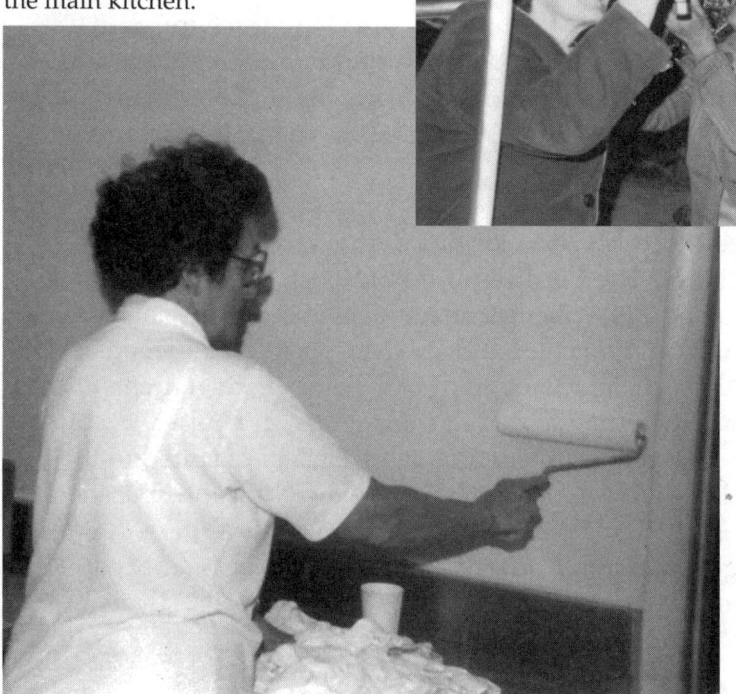

...e Starling, adding siding ...he main house.

Fred Hamby and Alline planting raspberry bushes.

...nley Langford, stonemason, ...ork.

Al Madison, heading a Bethany team in building a retaining wall.

Bethany work team, hoisting a section of deck into place.

Bob Flack, working on concrete floor slab.

A Bethany team, building an arched bridge.

A work team from Seminole, Florida helped on the new shop building.

Harold Carlson and Clayton Harder on the fifty-foot bridge they built

Ruth Ramey, cooking and helping in the work.

Porter Harris, our master plumber.

kitchen utensils, as well as many other items and sent them to us. She never knew how much she contributed to the furnishing and outfitting of our five kitchens and other areas of the retreat.

My mother, Beth Hanson, is a good seamstress. In those early days she usually came down from Iowa once a year. She loved to put her skills to work. During one such visit, despite the fact that she was in her seventies, she turned some 160 yards of cloth into drapes and other items. We were so grateful for this tremendous help.

No one can surpass the Lord in finding unique ways to supply needs. We received a call from the pianist at the Baptist church we were attending. She also happened to be the postmistress in a nearby town. She told us that her husband had been driving along one day behind a National Linen Service truck. A large bag of linens fell off the top of the truck and landed on the highway. Her husband stopped, picked it up and brought it home. They contacted the linen service to tell them that they could pick up their bag of linens at the post office, but they never came for it. So the lady called us and said that she had laundered the sheets and pillow slips, and that she would like for us to have them for the work here!! So, if you visit us and see a sheet stamped National Linen Service on its hem, you will understand that it was a miracle, not theft which brought us this supply of sheets!!

Bethany Missionary Church in Minneapolis, my home church, has been used of the Lord for a number of years to do a great job of refurbishing buildings, painting, doing grounds work, cleaning, remodeling, roofing and building bridges.

This work team is made up of the senior teen youth who call themselves "Action For Teens." A group of the skilled maintenance men from the staff of Bethany Fellowship accompanies the young people to lead and oversee the projects. Jan Easterday has given many hours of service organizing the team, helping to make preparations for the meals, and serving as overseer of the girls' work. Harold Carlson has used his carpentry and electrical skills to very good purpose here. Al Madison, Glen Hofer, Lee Ray, Ron Asmus, Jim Dahlen, and many others have poured out energy and effort to build up the facilities and improve the grounds. More recently, a team of college-age young people from Minnesota came to work on urgent projects. We can never thank the Lord enough for their willingness and their efforts.

When we first came to the retreat, our main dining room had very little furniture in it. There were two sway-backed, picnic-type tables, fifty-two children's school desks, and no chairs. You can imagine our joy when Bethany Fellowship brought a truckload of sixteen circular dining tables and one-hundred fine chairs for the dining room. It was a red-letter day for us!

We still needed dishes and silverware to serve the groups we envisioned coming to our retreat. In the Lord's timing, a Christian couple closed their restaurant nearby. They gave us over fifty restaurant-quality plates, dozens of soup bowls, platters, salad bowls, glasses, silverware, a salad bar, a serving counter, and a lovely light fixture to hang over the buffet table. What a transformation these items brought to our dining room!

Russell and Florence Marble met Alline in the Philippines and then followed her further adventures in our newsletter, *The Boondocks Bulletin.* In 1983 they stopped in to see what we were doing here in north Georgia during our early days in the Valley. They had worked on the mission field, helping set up telephone systems. So when they came to visit us, they saw immediately that we needed an intercom system to connect our various buildings and save much running back and forth. So they went home with that challenge on their hearts and began to organize a team of Bell telephone retirees in their church. They returned to install a fine system of phones. Jim and Helen Henderson, a retired Bell couple living in Michigan, joined them. In recent years, Jim has come a number of times to repair and upgrade the system to keep it in operation. Un-

Richard Wood, mowing.

Ray and Lois Veenker, two of our missionary helpers.

Mildred Swope, cleaning windows.

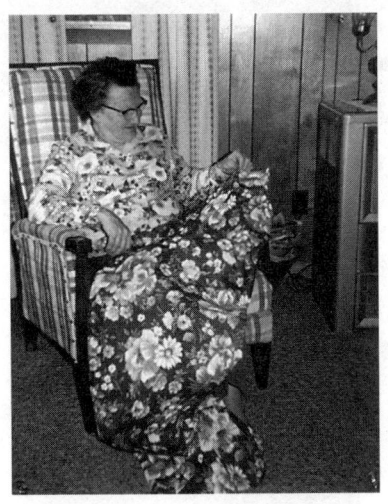

Beth Hanson, making drapes.

Jan Easterday catered the Bethany work team.

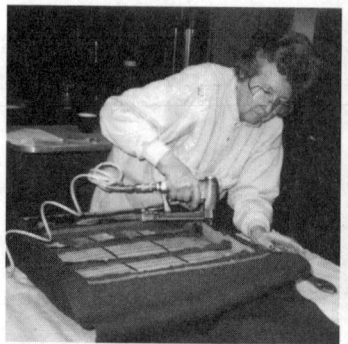 

Florence and Russell Marble have done invaluable work upholstering chairs and other furniture.

Richard Wood, Dee Hurm, and Wayne Prosser, standing on the new deck for the dining and meeting room.

Elease Nicely, caterer.

Jim Henderson, helping lay underground cable for our intercom system.

derground cable for this project was donated by the technical arm of Wycliffe Bible Translators, JAARS. Phones came from T.A.P., a missions technical service in California. Our local telephone company has been of great assistance to us also. We are so grateful for all who have helped make this project a reality.

Several years ago, a group called The Telephone Exchange in Ohio donated a new intercom system to the work. We thank these friends for this excellent equipment to upgrade our phone service.

Even in their retirement years, the Marbles have been vigorous and busy helping in the work here. They decided to take a course in upholstery as a hobby, but it turned into a full-time business. They have graciously used their skills to help us. In one visit they upholstered nineteen lounge chairs for our meeting area. During other visits they re-covered two couches and two Lazy Boy chairs. Florence has also used her skill as a seamstress to make drapes for our large meeting/dining room and to make curtains for other rooms. How we thank the Lord for the contributions of the Marbles.

We wore many hats in our early days at Fellowship Valley. One of them was "motel maid." Alline and I washed more sheets, made more beds, and cleaned more bathrooms than we could number. We were "it" until the Lord had mercy on us and brought us a wonderful team member to lift our load. Ruth Ramey, a speedy and efficient house cleaner, came to us just in time. How we thank the Lord for her willing spirit and for her very long hours of hard work as our co-worker, helping to keep the facilities ready for guests and groups.

In 1991, another retired couple came to Fellowship Valley in answer to the Lord's prompting. At an age when most people would be leading a fully retired life, they came to do a full-time job. Bea and Evan Grahn had served for years in Senegal, West Africa, with WEC International.[1] They came to us when

---

[1] Formerly Worldwide Evangelization Crusade.

Two Weak Women

Evan and Bea Grahn were a gift from the Lord to the ministry as they asisted with maintenance and the care of our guest facilities as well as enjoying the work with international students.

we urgently needed a maintenance man. We had been praying for years for God to send a spiritually mature couple to work with us, the husband for maintenance work and the wife to care for guest accommodations. When Evan and Bea arrived, Evan said that he didn't want to be a preacher. He just enjoyed doing maintenance. His wife, Bea, said that she loved to clean and make beds! What a perfect answer to prayer! They gave dedicated, loving service for a year and a half before finding it necessary to retire fully.

These are rare gems, the Lord's special servants who walk in obedience to His leading and give of themselves to do whatever the Lord indicates. They are co-laborers with us, and we thank God for each of them. They will see in heaven the full fruit of their labors.

In the early 1990s, we began to see some progress in the realization of our dreams for new buildings. The Bethany Fellowship team laid half of the slab for the new shop and maintenance building—a place where we could finally keep our tools and equipment in one spot! For fifteen years, we had stored them in several different buildings, and often it was a puzzle to know where to find the correct tool when a workman came to help.

Bob Flack, Harold Thompson, and Jim Wiess finished the slab and went on to frame up the building. In a matter of days, we were watching the crane lift the trusses into place for the roof. Then Harold and Arthur Chambers put on the roofing.

A group from Sun Coast Bible Church in Seminole, Florida, under the leadership of Dee Hurm, came to finish the inside of the building, including the electrical work. What a day it was to see our dream—the workshop—become a reality.

His name is Porter Harris. He is a master plumber, and he plumbed for years for the Master here at Fellowship Valley. He has answered more SOS calls than we can count as we have experienced emergency after emergency: broken pipes, frozen pipes, underground water line breaks. He has faithfully and graciously responded to our calls and kept us operating. Porter is 82! His reward is going to be special when he meets his Master!

In 1995 the Lord sent us another special gift. Richard Wood, my cousin, came to help us with the grounds and maintenance work for three months. He has done many urgent tasks: painting buildings, helping with construction, tending the grounds, assisting with our guest units in various ways, making repairs, and in general using his gift of helps to make himself invaluable to the ministry. He has also had a part in leading the services for international student retreats. He uses his gift in music for choir, solos, and for leading song services in the local church he attends. At the end of his three-month stay he felt led to continue helping indefinitely. We are so thankful for his presence and help in the work.

Many other willing workers have come, like Wayne Prosser, a skilled carpenter and missionary builder. Phil Shappard also used his skills to help remodel buildings. Phil is now director of satellite communications for Moody radio in Chicago. We have seen a new staff house set up and many volunteers had a part in that project, like our stonemason friends, Manley Langford and his brother, Lewis, and Maurice and Georgia Starling. Warren Bell, retired from IBM, has contributed a great deal by using his skills to help us with computer problems. We cannot thank the Lord or these people enough for all that they have done for this work. Without them, we would not be here ministering to the churches of the southeast or to the far corners of the world through the international student ministry. We could not carry on if it were not for the many volunteer workers!

12

"When I Am Weak"

Corrie ten Boom occasionally visited the mission headquarters of Christian Literature Crusade when Alline and I served there. C.L.C. was Corrie's publisher long before her book *The Hiding Place* came out. She happened to be in our headquarters in 1974 just as Alline was preparing to leave for Georgia to ready herself for service in the Philippines. It was the custom for the mission family to hold a farewell dinner for outgoing candidates. We had all gathered one evening for this purpose. After dinner, various staff workers stood up and gave

Author Corrie ten Boom and friend at Alline's farewell supper.

a Scripture verse or word of encouragement to Alline to carry with her into her new work. Corrie stood to her feet to give such a word. "When you get to the Philippines, you will have trials, testings and temptations," she said, "but remember this, God has no *problems*, only *plans!* There's no panic in heaven!" And Alline adds in retrospect, "Corrie was right. When I got to the Philippines I had trials, testings and temptations."

The trials were not long in coming. In fact, she didn't even have to wait to get to Asia! The next day, Alline packed her aging Buick to start for Georgia, and it was PACKED! She really needed a heavy man to sit on the trunk lid to make it close. In the first twenty-four hours of her trip south she had FIVE flat tires! That must be some kind of a record.

Alline's penchant for flat tires followed her even on her way *back* from the Philippines. When the jumbo jet landed in Dubai in the Persian Gulf, *it* even had a flat tire!

I liked to tease Alline that she went to extraordinary lengths to obtain exciting news for her letter to her prayer partners. Her first wild adventure in Manila certainly confirmed that. Alline and two other missionaries were walking down a dark side street on their way to a bus stop one evening. They were walking in the street next to the curb because there was no sidewalk. Suddenly, they realized that headlights were bearing down on them from behind. The others scattered left and right, but Alline was left stranded in the middle. As the car passed Alline, hands reached out of the rear window of the car and grabbed her shoulder bag. Alline could not release it because she had been carrying it with her thumb hooked through the metal ring which held the strap to the bag. As soon as the stranger in the back seat took hold of the bag, the car accelerated rapidly. Alline was swept off her feet and literally *dragged* along on the rough pavement as the car raced forward! She thought to herself with incredulity, "This can't really be happening to ME!! This only happens in *movies!*" Then the car made a sharp turn onto the main street of Manila, still dragging its hapless victim. It was a miracle Alline wasn't run over

"When I Am Weak"

as the car made its turn. Suddenly, the strap was either cut or it broke, releasing her to fall into a crumpled, bloody heap on the street. She was dazed; her clothes were torn. Meantime, her missionary friends were searching desperately for her in the dark, wondering what had become of her. When they finally found her, she was in a state of shock. Mercifully, one of the missionaries was a nurse and was able to obtain medicines to treat her wounds before taking her home. It took a month for her to recover. Later the police caught a band of thieves who had been preying on tourists at that corner.

Unusual escapades commonly occur in Alline's life. In the years since she has come to Fellowship Valley, she has continued her pattern. One day she was on the roof of one of our lakeside cabins helping Ruth and Dock Ramey put a new layer of roofing material on the roof. Because the center area had been leaking badly, they stripped the roof away completely and opened a hole for a new sheet of 4'x8' plywood. Alline was standing on the roof receiving 2'x4' boards from Dock, who was on the ground. She kept stepping back and back to handle longer boards. Suddenly, she stepped backwards into thin air, through the opening in the roof and began to plummet downward into the cabin! Wildly, she grabbed for something to break her fall. Again, angels helped her find a grip on each side of the opening, and there she hung in midair, eight feet above the cabin floor. Ruth and Dock rushed to hold her and help her down.

In recent years, Alline has changed over from continual flat tires to numerous broken bones. She counts eight broken bones since returning from the Philippines. One day she came down to the area near the lake where we had just torn down an old storage shed. She was talking to a man who was helping us when suddenly she stepped on a long, ugly roofing nail. It pierced her thin tennis shoe and penetrated her foot. She leaped into the air in excruciating pain! When she came down she landed on her other foot and broke a bone in it! So for weeks, she was hobbling around first on one foot, then on the other!

"The woman is the man for the job," was the saying in our mission where male workers for the fields were all too often in short supply. So one day here at the retreat, Alline was doing a man's job. She had "Amazing Grace" parked on a short slope in our back driveway and she was up in the bed of the truck. She was using all of her strength to wrestle a section of the heavy wooden sideboards into their fastening position. The whole massive board structure suddenly went out of control and pitched over the side onto the hard, red clay embankment below the truck taking Alline with it! She fell with a terrible crash to the ground. Injured and in great pain, she struggled to drag herself about two hundred feet, then up our back stairs to the kitchen door, where she collapsed and called for help. She was already going into shock.

I was sitting in the living room in utter weakness, having just returned home from the hospital. I had suffered a heart spell shortly before this and my heart kept going out of normal rhythm. Two efforts to shock it back into normal rhythm had

One of our weaker moments.

not corrected the problem. As I heard Alline's cry for help I summoned all of my adrenaline and rushed to her aid. Somehow, we succeeded in getting her to a chair in the living room. I packed her rapidly swelling knee in ice. Alline thought she had merely aggravated an old basketball injury so she did not feel that it was necessary to see a doctor. In the days following her accident she hobbled around on crutches, hiding her misery.

Then I had to return to the hospital and Alline was visiting me when my doctor came in on his rounds one evening. He immediately gave orders for Alline to come to his office for an X-ray the next day. They found that the knee cap had a small piece broken out of it. She spent weeks in a cast and on crutches. Then she worked on a stationary bike to regain her mobility.

My heart problems left me short of energy for the strenuous days of work we had before us. I fell into periods of deep exhaustion on an almost regular basis. I would go to my doctor feeling like a wilted plant and he would say to me, "Bonnie, you need to learn to delegate." Well, that would have been very nice but there were only *two* of us. So I had to delegate to Alline and she would delegate to *me!* That didn't really solve my problem of exhaustion.

Early in our time at Fellowship Valley, we had a helper named Violet Jack. She was a bit older than we were and had some physical problems, too. Nevertheless, she was lifting and carrying heavy lumber and furniture right along with the rest of us. One day she received a letter from her daughter in New York. She said to Violet, "Are you still having those weak spells?" Laughingly, Violet replied, "I forgot I ever *had* a weak spell!!" Our local pastor re-named her "The Incredible Hulk!" (You will see Violet's photo in the picture section—The "Hulk" in action.)

Shakespeare said that all the world is just a stage, and we are but the players. I do believe that some of us are destined

Two Weak Women

Violet, the "Incredible Hulk," helping to move a refrigerator.

to make many of our moves on *center* stage. Alline is one of those.

We had a building project in progress at the retreat, and it fell to Alline to return a load of unusable insulation and paneling to the lumber company. It was stacked high on our pickup truck, and she started off to town. I was leading the way in our car because we had business to do at the bank and were to meet there before she went on to the lumber company. We arrived at the stop light on the square in the heart of downtown Clarkesville. It is a place where two major highways meet, so traffic is heavy at that intersection. The light turned green and I proceeded down the street toward the bank, believing that Alline was right behind me. I parked behind the bank and went inside to wait. As time went on and Alline did not appear, I was mystified. Finally, I went out the front door of the bank, down to the edge of the street, and looked back up Main Street toward the square. I was horrified to see a disaster in progress! There, in the middle of that busy intersection I could see our huge bats of insulation lying scattered on the street and the pickup truck sitting at an odd angle. Convinced that Alline had been in a collision I rushed to the car and raced back up the street. When I arrived, I found indeed a pile of both insulation and paneling lying on the street. Alline might as well have been a Southern lady decked out in hat, summer dress, and gloves looking calmly over the scene for all the excitement she displayed. She was standing there looking on unruffled while several chivalrous men rushed about hauling the insulation bundles and boosting them back onto the truck for her. Smiling and unflustered as though this were an everyday occurrence, she reassured me that all was well. Apparently when she had started up the truck to move on through the green light behind me, the weight of the insulation was too much for the ropes holding the bundles. They snapped! The insulation and paneling flew into the air and scattered into the busy intersection, bringing traffic to a halt. No one was hurt. There is no panic in heaven!!

Alline really got a "charge" out of a summer thunderstorm we had! She was sitting on the couch near the phone. One of our cats was curled up on her lap. Suddenly, lightning struck and a bolt came into the living room with a sharp explosion! It blew out the bulb in the lamp next to Alline, severed the telephone wire on the wall about three feet from Alline's leg. (She felt the tingle as it passed by.) It then jumped over into the intercom wire next to the phone and exploded about five times causing spurts of little colored wires to erupt out of the line. But the thing Alline felt most was the claws of the cat as the initial lightning bolt exploded in the room. The cat literally took off into mid-air—but not before she, in terror, had dug her claws into Alline's leg! After the lightning struck, we smelled hot wires, but there was no fire. We thanked the Lord for His protective hand.

Corrie ten Boom's word to Alline is a good word for me, too. In 1992 we had a very heavy season of groups which continued until early December. Other work kept me running. So when January came, I was so weak and exhausted that I could scarcely move from my bed. The doctor could not find a problem and so for weeks I lay there. A return visit to the doctor

Two Weak Women

in February brought a surprise. He discovered that my heart was enlarged and had me admitted to the hospital. After a brief period of observation, he noted that my heart rate had dropped to about twenty-eight beats a minute. (Sixty to one hundred is more normal for most). Within hours he had me transported by ambulance to Emory University Hospital in Atlanta where a heart pacer was inserted into my chest. Now I laughingly say that I am finally able to "pace" myself. The pacer has helped a great deal in my ability to keep going in our rush of work and I do thank the Lord for that.

You would begin to think that I loved hospitals when I tell you that I was in again within a short time. But this visit was caused by a tick bite! We had just begun to hear on the national TV news of the dangers of deer ticks and the Lyme disease they spread when I noticed a large, circular bite on my leg. Tests were done but by the time the results were in I had to be hospitalized for ten days for intravenous drug treatment for Lyme disease. Some months later I received another tick bite, but this time it was diagnosed quickly so that I could be treated with oral medication.

During one of the times when Alline had a broken bone in her foot, I was trimming the high weeds on the earthen dam.

"When I Am Weak"

Alline was sitting on the golf cart nearby as I gingerly made my way down the face of the dam, carrying long clippers in one hand. Suddenly my feet went out from under me (I had forgotten about the morning dew on the grass). I reached out my left hand to catch myself and fractured my upper arm! Alline and I made a comical team as we went around—she limping and I with one arm in a sling. Not to worry, "The lame take the prey," Isaiah tells us.

Physical problems can be quite a test of faith if you do not carry health insurance. I have always been the weaker one, with many physical problems. The finances needed for endless doctor bills, tests, and hospitalizations during those early years had to be met in miraculous ways. And God met them, praise His name!

In 1981 it was necessary for me to have a cataract removed. The Lord not only gave me the director of an eye hospital as my surgeon, but he also performed the operation without charging his fee. His wife was a friend of Alline's from school days, so they invited us to stay with them in their home during my surgery time. That spared us the expense of a motel, as well as being a very nice gesture on their part. I was the only patient in town who had a doctor who made house calls! Following that surgery I needed new glasses which would cost nearly $200. I hesitated to make an appointment for the eye exam, but Alline urged me to go ahead. I did, and just four days before the appointment, I received a letter from someone I had never heard from before, nor since. In the letter was a check designated for my medical expenses! The check was for $200. "God has no problems, only plans. There's no panic in heaven!"

With every broken bone there comes a sizeable medical bill. And sure enough, right after Alline fell down the steps of a friend's home and broke her leg, the bill came. Its arrival set the stage for our El Shaddai ("the more than enough God") to perform another miracle in our behalf. The friends in whose home Alline fell informed us that they carried home owner's insurance. We were very thankful to learn about this. But the story does not end there! Strangely enough, the insurance company insisted upon sending a check for $500 dollars, though the medical bill was less than $200. So we sent the balance to our friends, since it was rightfully theirs. Soon afterwards, we received this unforgettable note from the husband:

> Some people are so lucky. When they break their bones in other people's houses, and other people's insurance company pays them for their pain and suffering as well as their out-of-pocket medical bills, and they send the pain and suffering money to the other people, and the other people consult the insurance company about it, and the other people's insurance company promises to let them know something if it should be returned to the other people's insurance company, and the other people's insurance company never responds to the other people any further, and the other people clearly see from this that the pain and suffering money should stay with those who underwent the pain and suffering, and the other people send the check for the pain and suffering money back to them that broke their bones, and ask them to divide it half to them that broke their bones and half to them that lived with them that broke their bones and took care of them and had pain and suffering along with them that broke their bones. How lucky can some people get?

Along with this classic message came a check for $300! It was just what we needed to pay for a trip we had to make to a missions conference in Pennsylvania! What unusual ways the Lord has to meet our needs! Thank you, Lord.

It was *almost* panic for Alline the year her cook, Bonnie, left to spend Christmas in Iowa. She was left alone to take care of one guest who would be with her over the holidays. This lady was also a Southerner, so it seemed like it would be an easy situation. They had a good supply of greens, black-eyed peas, and grits on hand. All was well . . . for the moment. For some folks cooking is not a strain, but Alline had been raised in a home where she had not had to learn to cook.

"When I Am Weak"

The Christmas rush should have eased off once Christmas eve arrived. But for Alline, it was like the start of a one-hundred-yard dash. She was "home, home on the range," (the gas range, that is) as the chief cook, and life took on an extra dimension of stress for her.

The phone rang just before Christmas, and soon the guest list was expanded by *three!* The mad rush to strip sheets and make beds, clean a cabin, prepare meals, and play the well-composed hostess kept Alline on the stretch for the next couple of days. By the morning of the second day, she had run out of menu ideas! So it was back to the *I Never Cooked Before Cookbook* and the canned goods supply!

The first wave of company left to continue their journey, but on the 27th three *more* visitors arrived! These were expected guests, but once again the hostess went into a whirl to prepare rooms and meals while sandwiching in tours to Toccoa Falls, Tallulah Falls, and the town of Helen. On January 2nd, the regular cook returned from vacation. Yes, I believe that was a sigh of relief I heard.

During the 1980's Alline had a new responsibility come to her. She fell heir to the full-time care of two elderly aunts. A double-wide home was duly installed on our retreat property for them and they moved in. Alline began to try to divide her days between pressing retreat work and the needs of the two weak, dependent ladies. She sought live-in help but it was a continual problem as helper after helper came and went. More and more of Alline's time had to be spent in their care. So the load of retreat tasks had to be shifted somewhat and we moved on in His strength "faint yet pursuing," as the Word says. (The elder aunt passed away at a hundred and one and the other at eighty-eight.) Those were good years of preparation, for now Alline has the care of her mother who is ninety-three.

We two weak women came to Fellowship Valley when we were fifty. It was foolish in the natural to launch into such an undertaking at that age. But then we have a God who does unusual things. So, thirteen years later, it was no surprise that

He also brought along Hanna Foerster and Emma Wisser who are also in their "prime!!" Hanna was then a couple of years older than we were, and dear Emma was *seventy-seven!!* Hanna had served for over thirty years in Liberia and The Gambia and Emma had served for *fifty-one* years in these two countries. We began to have a "family" joke that we are called "the over-the-hill-gang!" And Alline smilingly adds, "Yes, over the hill and picking up speed!!"

We have no plans for retirement. We still have so much to do to reach the goals God has given. One of our staff has expressed a desire to be buried here on the retreat grounds when she is called "home." So we decided to set aside a special plot of land, and put a nice fence around it. Over the gate we will put a sign which reads, "Fellowship Valley Retirement Center."

13

A Merry Heart

A good sense of humor is essential to life and service. We have had plenty of laughs in our dilemmas and crises.

It was a balmy, summer night. The hour was about two in the morning. Our living room door was open to let the cool, night air waft through the house. This same door led out onto a flimsy porch roof which clung to the front of our house. There was no screen door, but we were not bothered with mosquitoes here in the mountains.

Alline had been asleep for hours when suddenly she was shocked out of her dreams by a horrendous smell in her room—in her *bed!* She sat up bleary-eyed and looked around, sniffing the air. SKUNK!!

It was a *skunk!* Then she spotted our black-and-white lady cat curled up in her blankets and leaned over to sniff her fur. SKUNK! The cat had been close to a skunk and then had crawled up the porch post, come in the open door, and crawled blissfully into bed with Alline! Lady Cat was snatched out of her dreams, out of her comfy place in the blankets, and unceremoniously deposited outside, and the door was *shut!* For days to come, the cat could not understand our sudden "cold shoulder" toward her.

Somewhere along the way Alline had seen a do-it-yourself TV program on bee keeping. She decided it would be fun to try it out. Just think of all that tasty honey the nice little bees would create. She prepared the hives and the frames for the honey, and then set up two hives in the woods behind our house. She looked quite the part of a beekeeper in her wide-brimmed bee bonnet with the netting tied securely at her neck, working her "smoker" to quiet the bees. All was going well, and she dreamed her dreams of the honey harvest to come. (I was wondering more about the sticky mess that comes with honey extraction!) It was just a minor disaster the day she didn't have her bonnet tied quite tight enough and a few bees got inside. She was suddenly wild in her desperation to escape. I tried frantically to help her, and we both fled toward the house, the bees following and stinging us repeatedly. You've all heard the phrase about having a bee in your bonnet? Well, let Alline tell you, it's no fun!

Out in the forest on our fifty-five acres, someone else was dreaming similar dreams about the honey harvest. One morning I went to the retreat dining room and discovered a mystifying scene on the driveway behind the building. A creature (of some size, I surmised) had dragged our garbage barrel and scattered the contents widely, even up the drive toward the woods. When I returned to our house, I noticed that the bee hives were knocked over and the honey frames strewn around and broken. The bees were in an utter state of trauma. I rushed to tell Alline. It didn't take long to realize that we had had a visitor the night before. His name was obviously Winnie the Pooh!!

We called the Georgia State Game Commission to get professional help. They brought a huge, steel bear trap and parked it next to the bee hives. It was like a huge steel culvert on trailer wheels. Welded steel mesh covered one end and a trap door the other. The trap was baited with meat; then we waited. At dusk we were watching from my bedroom window when "Winnie" appeared. He walked around the cage sniffing for

the meat, then took the only way into the enclosure to get it. As he grabbed the bait, the trap door released itself behind him. We had caught a BEAR!! He only weighed 225 pounds, but he was ill-tempered, and I was glad I had never met him out in the woods. Alline bravely tried to take photos of him in the cage, but every time she inched close and got her lens aimed between the mesh strands, he would lunge at her, spraying her with his spit. It scared her and threw her back on her heels, but she persevered until she finally got some pictures.

These will never appear in The National Geographic!

That night was filled with the angry crashing and thrashing of the bear in his metal prison. I wondered if it would hold him until the ranger arrived the next morning. It did, and the ranger took him to the mountains north of us and released him.

Exactly seven years later, one of his relatives came by to check out our honey supply. *He* was *325* pounds! We managed to trap him also, and the ranger took him to Warwoman Mountain north of us and released him into the wilds. We have seen *evidence* of other bears but have never actually seen any more. Alline gave up her bee-keeping hobby after the second bear destroyed the hives. We never had so much as a *taste* of honey from that dream project!

The early 1990s seemed to be the era of the skunk in Fellowship Valley. Our senses were assailed again and again by the unspeakably awful odor of these animals as they paraded past our home, got into the basement through a door left open, or were frustrated as they tried to pry open a garbage barrel behind our house.

The worst moments came when they invaded the crawl spaces of our guest accommodations through seemingly tiny openings around air conditioner pipes in the foundations. Our helper, Arthur Chambers, courageously crawled under the first home to attempt an eviction of a skunk. He deserved a medal for bravery. One false move and he could have been stained with that horrific spray. He used a chemical under the house and worked other schemes to drive the visitor out. Finally, the skunk got the message and scuttled out from under the house. But before we realized what was happening, it scurried around the house and dove through a small hole in the foundation of the *next* house, and we found ourselves back to square one! Worse yet, we discovered there was not just one, but TWO guest houses filled with skunk odor! And we needed to have the houses ready for a retreat group in a few days.

Arthur gingerly opened the crawl-space door under the second home and crept in to do battle. This skunk was even more difficult to evict. But determined, Arthur kept at it with chemical sprays and made life so unpleasant for the skunk that it finally decided to leave. When it did at last move on, Arthur rushed to caulk up similar holes in the foundations of the other two guest houses nearby to avoid future problems.

But the battle was not over! One day as I was driving up Hanna's and Em's driveway on the golf cart, I was surprised to see the two of them standing in an unusual pose in the doorway of their house. Hanna was poised with a section of four-by-four lumber held high overhead. She appeared ready to plunge it down on the critter cowering on the ground below her porch. Em was right behind her, peeking around her. When Hanna saw me approaching, she cried out, "What IS this thing?"

I got off the golf cart and walked in a wide circle to take a look. Then *I* got excited! "Don't DO it, Hanna," I cried out. "It's a SKUNK!" Hanna and Emma quickly backed into the house. What a narrow escape from a smelly disaster! A trapper told us that skunks do not die easily. Even if you shoot them or kill them in some other way, they will leave their awful "calling card" for you to remember them by! Hanna, a native of Germany, was not familiar with our wildlife!

One night soon afterward, Hanna awoke in the night feeling sick. There was a terrible odor in the air which made her feel awful. It seemed to originate under their bedroom. The next morning we found that once again a skunk had found a little opening near the air conditioner outside and was in happy residence under their house. We called in a trapper, but he was not able to help without causing the skunk to emit its odor. Once again Arthur crawled under the house and met the creature face-to-face! He did his chemical attack on the creature and retreated. The ladies vacated their home, unable to live with the odor. Finally, the skunk took his leave and the hole in the foundation was promptly sealed!

Two Weak Women

The skunk saga continues right up to this day. One morning recently Alline walked out onto her back deck to put something into the garbage barrel. She lifted the lid and what should greet her but the surprised stare of two beady skunk eyes! Alline quickly slammed the lid down, but it was too late to spare her from a dose of her visitor's stench. Later in the day she fastened the barrel shut and put it on the pickup truck. She drove north on our gravel road up into the national forest near the gap in the mountains. There she dragged the barrel off the truck and tipped it over on its side at the edge of a cliff. Gingerly pulling the lid off and keeping carefully to one side, she tilted the barrel to dump her unwanted guest over the edge of the slope. But he was buried in a bag of garbage and so the garbage went with him down the embankment! So to retrieve her garbage Alline had to slide down the slope with the skunk and the garbage to get the trash. You can be sure that she came home smelling like a "rose!!"

Our corner of wild America has been a delight to us. (Apart from the skunk adventures!) We love the raucous calls of the handsome, pileated woodpeckers. But they are becoming scarcer as development proceeds around us. We loved having wild turkeys wandering through the woods behind our house and sometimes through the *front* yard. We now see less of them, too. But recently, Alline did have the thrill of seeing eighteen turkey hens crossing the gravel road. Deer find a haven here for part of the year, and we enjoy the does and their copper-coated fawns flecked with white. We wish it could remain this way forever, but civilization is unrelenting. There is pressure to pave the wonderfully nostalgic, dirt road which passes our house. It's too bumpy for cars and too dusty, they say.

We have never found our remote location lonely. We know that it is choice—chosen by the Lord for this special ministry to people pressured by city life and the current problems of modern society. We *need* to retain havens away from the maddening throng—places where people can feel the quietness and become still enough in His presence to hear His voice.

14

Deer Never Cry "Help!"

Forty-three retired missionaries came to visit us from Bradenton Missionary Village in Florida in October of 1993. Alline toured with them on their charter bus each day to show them the scenery and sights in our region. The rest of our team prepared meals and did other tasks.

On Tuesday evening our guests were arriving a few at a time in the main dining room for the evening meal. It seemed that each time someone came in from the driveway behind the dining room they heard a peculiar, high-pitched cry from the woods high up behind the building. People wondered at this sound. We had never heard anything like it before, but one of our local helpers in the kitchen mentioned that her husband said that *deer* sometimes make such a noise. We went on about our rush to settle our guests and serve the meal.

Following dinner we held a meeting where we shared the story of our ministry. Then we began the process of shuttling our guests to their cabins and housing in various parts of the retreat. And again we heard this strange, high-pitched cry up in the woods each time a car came up to the rear door to pick up some guests. I drove several ladies to a cabin near our house and as I stepped out of the car I heard the strange cry again, this time louder than ever. I marveled and wondered *what* could this possibly *be!!* The final guest to be transported to her housing was Mrs. Anthony Rossi. Alline and I drove her to Hanna's and Emma's residence across the road. As I stepped out of the car the loud call of "HELP" came clearly from the darkness across the lake. Mrs. Rossi said, "That's not an animal!" I shouted to Alline, "Someone must have fallen on the path across the lake!" and began to run in that direction. She followed me. We rushed up the face of the earthen dam and stood on the dam listening. The cry came again and I felt it was from the area off to the left in the forest. I began to run toward the bridge to cross over the neck of the lake. As I stood on the path at the edge of the forest I heard the cry again, but this time it seemed to come from a distance in the direction of the dining room. I rushed down the path in that direction as fast as I could go. When I got there I heard the cry and it seemed to come from the opposite direction. I rushed back the other way. I soon tired of this mad chase and went for help. The bus driver was in the dining room so I recruited him in the search. He and I stood at the edge of the forest and listened as the call came again. He shouted up into the woods, "Who ARE you?" "Margaret," came the faint response. "WHERE are you?" persisted the bus driver. "South of the camp and west of the road," came the reply. It was very accurate. The driver took another man and Alline with him and they hiked up into our nature trail system, finally arriving at the farthest point on the trail, a cul-de-sac. Here they found two lost, chilled lady missionaries, Margaret and Dorothy! It seems that they had gone for a little walk before supper, had become confused about the route and could not find their way back. The search team brought the ladies down out of the forest and we seated them in front of the heating stove and gave them hot chocolate to warm them. Their misadventure was no small thing on a chilly October night in the mountains. They could have suffered hypothermia later in the night. One of the ladies was not well, having just recovered from a stroke. The other missionaries had been praying as we had searched in the forest so there was much relief and thanksgiving when the two were found. As we related the news to Mrs. Rossi, she said to us with an amused smile, "Remember, *deer* never cry HELP!!"

15

You're on the Air!

Having come from a Christian literature ministry and knowing that the Lord could use good books to touch lives, Alline and I thought it would be a good idea to encourage people to read fine Christian books. Perhaps radio would give us an opportunity to present quality book reviews for that purpose. WRAF-FM, a 100,000-watt station at Toccoa Falls College, was just seventeen miles from us, so one day in the 1980's we headed to the station for a tour. As we walked around with our kind hostess, we shared with her some of our thoughts about doing book reviews. She suggested that we produce a pilot program and then talk to the station manager, Jimmy Rich. We met Jimmy soon afterward, and he had an even more amazing suggestion. He was hosting a program on which he interviewed missionaries and other leading Christians. He asked if we might be able to help him with this program. We would actually be conducting the interviews. It all sounded very exciting. We liked the idea and felt it was a challenge we should accept. The only problem was that we had never done ANY kind of radio taping before and didn't know where to start. But we did obtain a professional tape recorder. Then our friend, Ken Franklin, came into the picture to rescue us. He built a mixer for us which we could use to make proper radio tapes. A whole new education was thrust upon us.

We boldly launched out, setting up interviews with people whose stories we thought might be of interest and be a blessing to listeners. One of our first interviews was with missionary Carolyn Eckman. She and her husband, David, had worked for many years with the Christian and Missionary Alliance missions program in Irian Jaya. They had come to Toccoa on furlough when, suddenly, their lives changed completely. David was diagnosed with cancer during their furlough and then passed into the Lord's presence.

I will share Carolyn's tremendous testimony because it was such a blessing to many who heard it.

"The morning I came home from the hospital I went into the bedroom, closed the door behind me, and said, 'Lord, I don't ever want to go out of this door. I just want to stay in this room till I die, because I feel there is nothing more left for me.' Then I realized that I have four children, and *they* needed me. But more than that, God brought me to a revelation that death is not a wound that will heal. I waited for the healing to come, but it never came. The wound is still there, very definitely so. Sometimes it is so painful that I feel I can hardly breathe, because the sorrow is so deep. But the Lord showed me that this is not a wound that will heal, but rather, it is an *amputation!* Part of me has been taken away, and it will never grow back. When a doctor amputates a leg, we don't expect the amputated limb ever to grow back. I have seen people who have only one leg, who sit in a chair and feel sorry for themselves day after day and never do anything in life again.

"Just a couple of years before we came home to the States, a young man came to Irian Jaya. He had been wounded during service in the army. He had one good leg and one wooden leg that squeaked when he walked. We were determined that we would not embarrass him, so everything we planned to do while he was there we planned to do on flat ground. For picnics we made sure that we were close enough to the picnic area so that he could walk on flat ground. Everything we did was planned around his wooden leg.

"One morning he said to me, 'I'm going to climb the mountain today with all the nationals around me. I won't be back until night, but when I come back I will have reached the top of that mountain out by your house!' He came back later that night victorious! He said, 'I went all the way to the top with them!! I can *do* it!!'

"I've thought of that picture so many times. I am just like a person who has only one leg. If I plan everything around the fact that I have had an amputation, I can feel sorry for myself, and there will never be anything else accomplished through my life. But I have asked the Lord to teach me to get out into the race again and to be able to win! I believe that this is what God is doing for me every day, because every morning I pray and commit my ways to Him. I can truthfully say that every morning new mercies I see, because His faithfulness is very true to me in my life."

In the years since Carolyn's husband died, she has indeed been used of the Lord greatly. Not only does she travel and speak in women's conferences, but she was the Dean of Women at Toccoa Falls College. The Lord has also used her to found a residential home for missionary kids who remain here in the States for schooling while their parents continue their missionary work elsewhere in the world. For Carolyn, life is very full. Life can be abundant even with a "wooden leg."

Tracking down good testimonies for our radio program took us far afield to meet new people and tape their stories. We interviewed Delta Airlines Captain Joe Ivey. From him we heard the story of the Fellowship of Christian Airline Personnel. We met him on the concourse as he emerged from his plane, having just returned from an overseas flight. We interviewed him in an office at the Atlanta International Airport while jets thundered overhead.

We found many intriguing people to interview. We spoke to well-known, Georgia author and watercolor artist, John Kol-

Alline, interviewing conference speaker Major Ian Thomas.

Bonnie, taping a program with author Roy Hession.

lock. John shared with us as we sat in his art studio overlooking the pond on his picturesque property. We taped the testimony of former Falcon football player, Greg Brezina. We enjoyed recording the story of Rudy Atwood, who made "Heavenly Sunshine" his piano trademark on the Old Fashioned Revival Hour many years ago. We also listened with excitement to a man who shared with us his adventures in smuggling Bibles into Mainland China. Then there were three young Russian men who had escaped from Russia in the days of the Iron Curtain. We also had the privilege of meeting others like Harry Stamm whose nephew, John Stamm, and wife, Betty, were martyred in China many years ago.

We taped the personal stories of men like singer Frank Boggs, well-known Bible conference speaker Major Ian Thomas, and musician Dick Anthony.

We were challenged by the testimony of Dr. Helen Roseveare, a medical doctor who served in what was then known as the Belgian Congo. During the uprising by African rebels in the 1960s, she was cruelly mistreated, raped repeatedly, and beaten by her captors. As she walked through her own dark valley, the Lord put this question to her: "Can you thank me for trusting you with this experience even if I never tell you why?" Miraculously, she survived and has been greatly used of the Lord in sharing her testimony and in presenting powerful messages of life in Christ in various parts of the world. In the years following her retirement, Dr. Roseveare has been entrusted by the Lord with a new deep testing—cancer.

After many weeks of visiting a medical clinic for treatment, she saw other women stricken with this disease, and she had a moving insight. She suddenly realized that she could never have ministered to these suffering women with true understanding had she herself not experienced the same pain and burden that they were feeling. She was able to offer these women the same comfort she had found in Christ in her own struggle with cancer.

It would take many pages to tell of all the people from

around the world who shared their stories with us on tape. We believe that their testimonies were a blessing to many. We aired an interview with missionary Roy Deck, who was serving with Trans World Radio. He had been forced to return to the States because of Paget's Disease—a bone disorder which cripples very slowly. After his story aired over WRAF, we received a letter from a listener in South Carolina who told how her husband had suffered from the same disease. She felt she might be of service in directing this missionary to good medical help.

Some of our tapes were used by the late night station operator at WRAF—Frank Nagle, the "Night Watchman." He also used some of the tapes on another station in South Carolina. He aired the testimony of Carolyn Eckman in this way. Apparently, this tape went even farther afield, for Carolyn told us that she received letters from as far away as Virginia in response to her testimony. We shared our own testimony on the air concerning our physical trials. It was aired during the night. Alline received a letter from a pastor in South Carolina whom she had not seen for about fifteen years. He had heard our testimonies. His wife was about to have serious surgery and desired encouragement in the Scriptures.

Author, Eugenia Price and Bonnie Hanson.

One of the most unforgettable days in our radio ministry was the day we spent on St. Simons Island, Georgia, interviewing authors Eugenia Price and Joyce Blackburn. We enjoyed a very pleasant time with them, first lunching together at a local country club and then taping the interviews. When the taping was completed, Alline and I returned to our lodging at the Christopher House Retreat. We had scarcely gotten into our room when we became aware of the sound of rushing water coming from somewhere nearby. The director of the retreat was away, so there was no one to ask about the sound. We began to do our own investigation. Fellowship Valley maintenance "man" Alline led the way, and together we headed to the apartment next door. Finding it unoccupied, we went in. To our horror, we discovered a disaster in progress in the bathroom!! A stopper on the top of the faucet fixture on an old-fashioned bathtub (the kind up on four legs) had broken loose. Out of the hole two geysers shot high into the air. The floor was awash in at least a half inch of water. Only the old-fashioned high door sill on the tiled floor kept it from overflowing into the bedroom. Alline swung into action! Nevermind that she was still wearing her best clothes! She immediately put her ingenuity to work and clamped the palms of both hands down over the holes where the geysers were spouting. She persisted and forced all the weight and pressure she could muster with her hands. It was like trying to plug up a fire hydrant! The water spewed in all directions from under the palms of her hands, soaking her to the skin. Next, she tried closing off the flood by placing a brick over the geysers. This didn't work either. We had no idea where the main water cutoff was located, so there was nothing we could do to stop the flow. We began mopping furiously to keep the water from pouring out into the bedroom area. There we were, swabbing with mops and pail, alternately throwing down a small rug to soak up the water and wringing it into the tub. Finally, in walked Carl, the director, to rescue us. Here's a piece of advice: If you go on vacation, and if you have a maintenance man, "don't leave home without him!"

The humorous side of the radio ministry continued to flourish. On one occasion, we were traveling to Philadelphia when we decided to stop near Lancaster to see the large replica of the Old Testament tabernacle. After taking a very informative tour, we asked our guide if we might interview her because we found her to be a very interesting and knowledgeable person. We searched the nearby Welcome Center office building for a quiet office where we could conduct the interview. None was to be found. Everywhere we went there were noises and people. Finally, we noticed a large, janitorial closet off the main lobby. We gingerly poked our heads in. It was definitely large enough for the three of us, but then we noticed that the door was louvered, allowing noise to come in freely. So we moved farther into the closet and discovered a restroom. It was spacious enough to hold the three of us, but it didn't have exactly the right kind of "furniture." There was nothing to sit on except the toilet stool. We were determined, however, and brought a small table and two chairs into the crowded room. The lady tour guide was very accommodating and unabashed at the setting. So we set up our equipment as best we could and took our unaccustomed places. Our guest had the best seat and we sat on the chairs. The interview went well, and we doubt that anyone in our listening audience ever guessed the location of our "studio!"

During this same period, the Lord opened the opportunity for us to have another radio program on a secular station nearby. We used this program mainly for Bible teaching, but we also aired some of our interview tapes.

We thank the Lord for this privilege of presenting Christ and the testimonies of His choice servants to the general public. We believe that this exceptional and widespread ministry provided an additional benefit for our retreat work. The broadcasting scope of the station included parts of three states, and the name of Fellowship Valley was spread farther abroad than we could ever have imagined. We thank God for enabling us to become better known in the region through this unique means.

16

An Incredible Deal

Swept along by such a wonderful wave of miracles, we could scarcely catch our breath. Volunteer helpers had been coming individually and in groups to restore our run-down buildings. We two weak women were rushing along and helping as much as we could, but by August of 1982, I was near collapse physically. We were not only working on repairs, cleanup, and hostessing guests, but we also had two radio programs and two home, Bible-study groups each week which required a great deal of preparation.

One afternoon I came to the house exhausted and stretched out on our living room couch to rest. I was lying there musing and thinking, "Lord, we can't go much farther by ourselves. We need staff, but we have no living quarters for them if they come." It seemed that we had reached a dead-end. As I lay there pondering, the phone rang. It was our architect friend, Tom Gregory. We hadn't heard from him in a long time. He said to me, "I have an *incredible deal* to share with you!" This was 1982, the year of the World's Fair in Knoxville, Tennessee. A consortium of business men in Knoxville had purchased 120 two-bedroom, two-bathroom, modular homes. They had placed them on a large property near Morristown, Tennessee, to rent out as overflow guest space during the fair. The project had not gone very well, as was true of the fair itself. Now, as the fair was coming to its conclusion, the men were eager to sell the homes. They had paid $12,000 for the construction of each home and then had furnished them. Now they were asking $10,500 for each of them. "This would be instant housing for you!" exclaimed Tom. "They are well built," he continued. I was excited by all that he told me and shared it with Alline. We didn't have any money, but we had the One who has all the world's wealth! So we shared our excitement with a very small handful of close friends so they could stand with us in prayer to see what the Lord would do. About four days later, we received a call from a group who said that they would like to *buy* one of the homes for us!! We were elated! Then, about a week later, the phone rang late one evening. The call was from a family living out of state. *They* wanted to buy TWO homes for us, maybe even THREE! It was unbelievable and *very* exciting! These donors finally decided to buy two homes and then give us a gift of funds for the development of the home sites—the drilling of a well, and the placement of the septic systems. Then our architect sent his engineer to guide in the preparation of the sites. It was a thrilling time.

When the sites were prepared, the first home arrived from Tennessee. By now it was November, and we learned that the owners of the homes in Tennessee were planning to remove all security guards who were watching over the homes. We were concerned that our purchases not be vandalized, but the check to pay for the final homes we had ordered had not yet arrived from the donors. We knew the check was coming, however, so to insure the safety of the homes by immediate delivery, we decided to take a thirty-day loan at our bank. We had little knowledge of how to carry through this procedure, so we contacted a businessman friend. He said, "I will take care of it. You two ladies just go to the bank tomorrow at two o'clock and talk to the manager." We did. We signed the necessary papers, and then the manager said, "We (the bank) would like to make a gift to your work." He gave us a check which covered all but twelve dollars of the amount we would have owed them for

An Incredible Deal

interest on the loan! Praise the Lord! I had never heard of a bank doing such a thing. God covers every detail!

The two homes arrived safely and were set up on the prepared sites. Then a missionary couple called. They had heard about our project with the new homes and wondered whether we might allow them to purchase a home from the firm in Tennessee and set it up on our property as a furlough home. They suggested that when they were on the field we could use it as a guest house. We thought that plan would work well so home number four was brought to us.

It was essential to have a good well for the new homes, but wells are expensive. We called in a young well driller and he went to work. Twice he tried boring wells but could not find sufficient water. So he set up his drilling rig and began to drill. On and on he went. By the time he had reached about 250 feet and still had not found water, he was getting concerned. He came to us and asked whether or not he should try another location. We knew nothing about well drilling, but Alline thought that he should continue where he was. Later that afternoon he came to our house, and with a rather long face, said, "Ladies, I have some sad news for you." We waited to hear the worst. "You need a well that produces ten gallons of water a minute for those four homes," he said, "but I was only able to get you *thirty*," he ended with a mischievous grin. We think he must have hit an underground stream! The water supply is superabundant!

The next challenge was to find a cement-block worker to put concrete-block skirts around the base of these homes to protect the pipes against the winter cold. We searched around our county but could find no one who was free to come. Finally, I suggested calling a pastor we knew in South Carolina to see if *he* knew anyone we could hire for the job. When I called, he said, "Do you know that just yesterday there was a man in my office wanting to do a project for the Lord, and he is a STONEMASON!" The pastor brought Manley Langford to see us, and he caught the vision! He soon returned with his flatbed truck loaded with bags of cement, a pile of sand, a cement mixer, and a crew of young fellows ready to assist him. They had finished about one and one-quarter homes when we found a local cement worker to finish the job. The stonemason went on to construct a lovely stone base for our new gate sign, as well as build two decorative retaining walls at our retreat entrance. He later returned to make a very attractive, natural stone pool and waterfall behind our little mill with the water wheel. We then went on to create flower gardens around the pool and the mill.

This same stonemason is standing by to assist with the building of fireplaces and other stonework on the new buildings we plan to erect. How we thank the Lord for this willing, expert, and gracious volunteer.

Almost as soon as the homes were settled on their sites, a young man named Rod Starling offered to work as a part-time maintenance man. This fine, young fellow already worked at Georgia Power Company, but he gave us many hours of help when he came home in the afternoons. He was with us for two years. What a blessing, and what an answer to prayer!

With the new homes in place, our retreat ministry for church groups began in earnest.

17

Transparent as Cooking Onions

My, you are going to be lonely!" remarked a lady from Atlanta when she visited us during our first years at the retreat. She had looked at our new setting, a valley seemingly far from any civilization and surrounded by forest. It did appear very remote. Our nearest neighbor was about one-half mile up the gravel road from us. If she could see us now, trying to cope with the continual stream of visitors, volunteer helpers, and retreat groups, she would know that we don't have the *luxury* of getting *lonely!!*

We've discovered there's no use planning a day's schedule, for as surely as we get into our old work clothes, a car will turn in at the gate with a bevy of visitors who want to see the work. And so the hours are spent in fellowship, lunch, and a tour of the grounds. But we don't mind. This is what we are here for: to fellowship, minister, and encourage people in their walk with the Lord.

One of the most frequent comments we hear is, "My, it is SO quiet here." Yes, it *is* wonderfully quiet here. It's a perfect setting for those who feel pressured in their jobs and overwhelmed by their busy lives. The Lord makes His presence felt here, and we thank Him for the way His Spirit ministers to people when they come. Many arrive with aching hearts, suffering over a marriage breakup, a rebellious child, a lost job, or financial problems. As they have waited on the Lord, prayed, and found love and counseling, they have experienced release from bondage and new freedom in Christ. This is what makes our labor worthwhile—seeing the Lord work in lives to accomplish His purposes.

We have hosted a wide variety of groups from churches and Christian organizations. There have been women's prayer retreats, men's sessions for discipleship and prayer, deacons and pastors for planning and spiritual renewal, college and career groups, military wives from bases near Atlanta, missionaries for R and R, teenage retreats, senior citizens coming for rest and blessing. Also various individuals and couples have come for personal prayer, fasting and renewal.

One evening we were preparing dinner for guests. One couple had already arrived, and we were waiting for the others when a car drove in. I went out onto the deck to see who had arrived. A young woman stepped out of the car and called up to me, "What kind of a place *is* this?"

"It is a place where Christians come to spend time with the Lord," I responded. She ventured up the path toward the house, and I went down to meet her. She had driven all the way from south Florida in obedience to the Lord. He had told her to come to the mountains for personal retreat. But He had not told her *where* to go in the mountains. As she rushed along the highway nearby, she had noticed our sign but had kept on going. The Lord prompted her to turn around and come back to Fellowship Valley. She decided to stay the night with us. We settled her in a home and gave her supper. She stayed four days and gave herself to prayer, studied the Word, and listened to good tapes. She had a blessed time and declared to us upon her departure that her life was changed. Several years later she left her executive job. She is now in a Christian university preparing for God's next step for her.

A young man in cutaway jeans, high hiking shoes, and a Tee-shirt which read, "I drank beer at Billy's" came walking up our front lawn one day. In his hand he carried a case of books.

Strolling in fall leaves at the retreat.

A quiet time of fellowship by the lake.

The baptism of a Chinese-Indonesian in our lake.

Robert Pettit and the pastor of the Iranian church which holds a retreat in our facilities.

A Cambodian Church on retreat.

A pleasant setting for study of the Word of God.

A planning retreat for missionary workers.

A couples' class from First Baptist Atlanta.

A men's group coming together for prayer and study.

He was a student at George Washington University doing summer sales work—selling *Bibles!*

We invited him in for a cool, summer drink and chatted with him. Our maintenance helper, Mike, attempted to witness to him. We gave him a copy of Chuck Colson's book *Born Again* as he left. In December of that year, we received a letter from this young man. He said, "I can't thank you enough for how much you all have affected my spiritual life. Since my encounter with such trusting and faithful servants of the Lord, I really began to wonder about my role in life. And it soon became more clear to me as I read much of the New Testament and the Old. And when I sat down to finally read *Born Again*, it was obvious what I was lacking and clear what I needed. I truly believe in Jesus now, and I feel completely at ease with all the pressures of my life. It truly is a gift He has to offer us, if we only let Him into our lives. . . ."

Our encounter with this young man was not a coincidence, for he, too, had been prompted by the Lord to come up our remote gravel road that day. Even though he didn't know why he was coming, he was obedient to God's prompting, and the Lord was able to meet him and bring him to the knowledge of Christ as Savior.

We watch in amazement as the Lord brings groups of men and women who are eager to seek the Lord. In the fall of 1994 we hosted one group of fifty-three men, and soon afterward a group of sixty-four Christian Iranians. They brought with them fellow Iranians from California, New York, Tennessee, Georgia, and both of the Carolinas. They had a weekend of real blessing here. One forty-year-old Iranian man was saved and a mother of five was baptized in our lake on the Sunday morning. Two other Iranians were baptized in our lake at a later date.

We have seen others enter the waters of baptism here, also. One was a Chinese Indonesian and the other came from Colombia, South America. It is a joy to see lives changed and committed to the Lord.

There is a wide range of immigrant churches in Atlanta. Over 150 languages are now spoken in that city. There are churches formed by Liberians, Ethiopians, Chinese, Iranians, Nigerians, Koreans, Cambodians and many others. We have had the privilege of hosting groups for retreat from some of these churches.

In June of 1996 one of our regular women's groups decided to hold a retreat for their teen-age daughters. To these, they added a number of inner-city girls from Atlanta, bringing the number to thirty-six girls, aged eleven through the upper teens. Twenty-two staff workers accompanied the group. Our housing almost needed elastic walls to contain the crowd! We only had fifty-two beds at that time!

What joy there was on Friday night when twelve of these girls gave their hearts to Christ, eleven others returned to the Lord from a back-slidden condition, and about fourteen others raised their hands for prayer for other needs!!

On the heels of this teen group we received a team of college-age young people from Bethany Missionary Church in Minneapolis, Minnesota. There were six fellows and three young ladies. One man was a carpenter so he devoted his time to building a new set of steps on one of our cabins. The girls helped prepare meals, washed windows and assisted with grounds work. Most of the fellows worked on the cleanup of the debris left by the tornadoes which had battered us three years earlier.

The young people decided to spend their July Fourth holiday afternoon in a nearby resort town where they could see fireworks that evening. As two of the fellows were walking down the street, they witnessed a violent, domestic quarrel. A couple was yelling, pulling hair, and biting each other. The two Bethany fellows intervened, pulling the two apart and setting them on their way up the street. The Bethany men decided to walk along behind them. They had only gone a block when the fight erupted again. The two men grabbed the husband and thrust him against a tree. "You need to get right with *God!!*",

Our largest youth group ever—fifty-one.

A womens' group coming together for fellowship and growth in Christ.

they declared to the husband. Amazingly, he broke down and began to weep. At that point they were able to lead him to the Lord! Another man approached them and they led him to the Lord, too! Just as they were saying to him that there is joy in heaven over one sinner who repents, the heavens over them erupted into a blaze of fireworks! It was almost like an affirmation of what they had said.

We rejoice with the angels over all who have come to the Lord and look forward to the many who will come in the years ahead.

We have received many testimonials to the Lord's blessing along the way. Here is a sampling.

"I just had to write to let you know how much my visit to Fellowship Valley meant to me. God really used you and your home to bring me closer to Him, and I am convinced that you are living on Holy Ground. As you know, I had a real crisis situation at the school where I work when I got back home, but I had an enormous prayer chain going for me, and I'm glad you four were a part of it. God brought me through with hardly a scratch, and my faith in Him has increased even more."

"Thanks again for touching our lives . . . The Lord truly led us to you that Sunday . . . and I am happy He did."

"I loved being with all of you at the retreat. Since the retreat, so much has gone on in my life it is unbelievable! The Lord has been working me over and showing me some things that I trust will allow me to walk with Him in a new way. I know the Lord wanted me to bring these books home with me "accidentally" (if there is such a thing with the Lord) because it led me to read *Rees Howells, Intercessor*. There is so much in that book that allows us to see what a holy life means through knowing Christ. Very few get to this point of death. This is why we have so little power in the church today. Pray for me to be willing to yield myself more and more to His purpose.

"The time here has been wonderful!! It's been a time of restoration and renewing which was deeply needed."

"Thank you for all your sacrificial work to make the weekend such a blessing to each one. We knew we were standing on Holy Ground. God was glorified! Lives were changed! Praise the Lord!"

"Thanks for all you did to make the weekend such a success. It seems that everyone who attended has been experiencing victory this week. There have been numerous opportunities for us to witness of what we learned."

After hearing our Fellowship Valley testimonial story, one person wrote: "I came not knowing why this weekend, expecting good fellowship, quietness, good music, and teaching. I got all that, but it didn't really touch my need until you spoke this morning. I thank you for being God's mouthpiece. Your testimony was what God needed to break down the molded, crumbling walls that I have kept repairing. TNT (dynamite) from God in the form of your life and your sister's life in Christ. You have the difference that makes the crucified life real to others. Thank you for being as transparent as cooking onions for our Lord and Savior."

18

To the Ends of the Earth!

"Every major venture contains a moment when you must step off the cliff and stretch your wings toward the sky."[1] And so it was that the Lord added to our team two more "weak" women to do a task which was parallel to Abraham's expecting miracles from the Lord in his old age.

Hanna Foerster is a German nurse who helped pioneer The Gambia for WEC International and served there as field leader

Emma Wisser and Hanna Foerster head the international student ministry.

---

[1]T. Davis Bunn, *Florian's Gate* (Minneapolis: Bethany House Publishers, 1992), 39.

Two Weak Women

for many years. She concluded her missionary career in West Africa by translating the New Testament into the Mandinka language. Hanna served a total of thirty-two years in the countries of Liberia and The Gambia.

Her co-worker, Emma Wisser, spent fifty-one years in the same two countries. She typed the New Testament which Hanna had translated. Upon concluding this project, they felt a new moving of the Lord in their lives. This time they felt a burden to reach West Africans who had come to the United States to receive higher education. The Lord spoke to Hanna and Emma about discipling these young men and women and preparing them to return to their own people as ambassadors for Christ.

During their brief furlough at Bradenton Missionary Village in Florida, they stopped overnight at Fellowship Valley. They were on their way to the WEC headquarters in Pennsylvania. As they shared their new vision with us, we silently absorbed what they said. They did not know just where the Lord would have them set up their new work. They planned to carry on a retreat-type ministry, teaching the Bible and fellowshipping with the students.

When they went on their way to Pennsylvania, Alline and I discussed their vision. We wondered, "Why not *here?*" We felt this new outreach could well be carried on at Fellowship Valley. So when the ladies returned about a week later on their way back to Florida, we shared our thoughts with them. They laughed, and said, "The Lord told us already that this was the place. But we said to Him that we would not say anything to you. But rather, the word must come from you!" Now they felt they had the Lord's confirmation for their coming.

Alline and I have both had a long-term interest in international students, and we have realized the great opportunity this ministry presented. For it is while the students are in this country, away from cultural and family pressures, that they are freer to investigate and accept the teachings of Christianity. To reach such students with the message of Christ means that we have the privilege of discipling them and seeing them return as witnesses to their own people.

" 'The cream of the crop' come to the U.S. to study, reports HIS International. International students represent the top five percent of the people in their countries. Thirty-three current heads of state were formerly international students here in the U.S.A. Over the next twenty-five years, about forty percent of the students presently studying in the U.S. will become leaders in education, business, government, and the military in their own countries. Many students come from countries that restrict or do not allow Christian activity. Over 100,000 international students are trained in the U.S. each year. Missionaries typically reach the bottom fifty percent of the people in a country, many of whom are uneducated. The upper twenty percent in China, South Asia, and Islamic nations are almost completely insulated from the Gospel, regardless of the mission dollars spent. These are also the most unresponsive. Yet students from these nations are here and are reachable."[2]

Hanna and Emma moved to Fellowship Valley in March of 1991. We had a home to offer them both as a residence and a base for their work. Once they settled in, they began to visit colleges and universities. They first made contact with school officials, then invitations were sent to the students to attend weekend retreats geared especially to their needs.

Hanna and Emma had thought that their ministry would be chiefly to West Africans, but the Lord had other plans. He brought men and women from all over the world to sit under the teaching of the Word of God. The first groups were small, but soon they increased. We watched as the Lord blessed and enriched the lives of the students. Warm bonds of friendship were formed with them. Bible studies brought seasons of prayer and sharing of needs. Hanna and Emma were then able to counsel, encourage, and point them to Christ.

We marveled as we saw the panorama of countries repre-

---

[2] HIS International, Columbia, S. Carolina.

sented in these retreats. Over fifty-two nationalities have been in attendance, including Liberia, Nigeria, Zimbabwe, Kenya, Uganda, Mainland China, Sierra Leone, Great Britain, Korea, Taiwan, Japan, Malaysia, Laos, Cambodia, India, Sri Lanka, The Bahamas, St. Kitts, Jamaica, Haiti, Brazil, Mexico, Spain, Cameroon, Ecuador, Canada, Holland, Norway, Cuba, Poland, Ukraine, Syria, Equatorial Guinea, The Gambia, Kazakhstan, Uruguay, Czech Republic, Slovakia, Indonesia, the Philippine Islands, Germany, Hong Kong, Costa Rica, Peru, Colombia, Nepal, Gabon, Burma, Russia, Bulgaria, and Romania. What a joy to have contact with the whole world right here at Fellowship Valley!! What an opportunity to touch the world for Christ!

There is already much fruit from this outreach. A young Ph.D. in chemistry from Mainland China, engaged at the time in a chemistry project at Clemson University, came to a weekend retreat. Hanna was talking with him in the dining room on Saturday afternoon when she was called away to attend to other matters. She invited a nearby Nigerian student to continue chatting with the Chinese visitor. He did and was able to lead him to Christ. That night at the campfire service, the newborn Chinese brother testified that now he knew what it meant to have his sins forgiven and to know Christ as his Savior. He wanted to tell his parents in China what had happened to him and finally wrote them a letter. He didn't know what they would say. Imagine his joy when he received a letter from them saying that they, too, had become Christians!

A young woman from Bulgaria, with a Ph.D. in chemistry, attended a weekend session. She was spiritually hungry but did not make a commitment at that time. However, she made an appointment with Hanna to come back to talk, and Hanna had the joy of leading her to Christ. She is now back in her home country of Bulgaria.

A lady from Uganda came to one of the retreats and later was in need of help after she had undergone surgery. She had no one to care for her in her post-operative weakness. Hanna, a trained nurse, invited the Ugandan into her home, and cared for her. Hanna had the privilege of leading her to Christ.

A student from Malaysia received Christ during a visit here and is now back in her own country. A young student from Ecuador also became a Christian while at Fellowship Valley. A lady from Cuba, a married student, somehow registered by mistake for the singles' seminar which was held here one summer. But it was no mistake. She found Christ and promptly registered for the married couples' seminar the following week. There she found encouragement and deepening in her new life in Christ.

One Thanksgiving holiday, a Russian Jewish couple attended a retreat. They listened attentively to the messages, and afterward, Hanna led both of them to the Lord. She also presented them with Russian Bibles, and they were delighted to have the Word of God in their mother tongue.

In early May of 1996 a brilliant, young engineer from Colombia, South America had been invited to the retreat for international students. He had turned down the invitation from other Spanish-speaking students, feeling that he really did not need to come to such a weekend. But after the others had left to travel to Fellowship Valley, he began to realize that "something" was telling him to GO, GO, GO!! So finally he gave in to this "voice" in his mind, and drove to the retreat by himself. During the weekend he was wonderfully saved. We marvel at the grace and persistence of the Holy Spirit, for this young man had completed his studies in the United States and would be leaving for Germany in just ten days to begin a final phase of work at the University of Heidelberg before returning to Colombia. Hanna, a German, contacted friends who would see that the young man was put in touch with a good church during his time in Germany. And when he returns to Colombia, she will be able to assist him in the same way through missionary friends there. Praise the Lord for this young man who can take Christ to his own people.

During the international student retreat weekend at the

of May, five Chinese students came to Christ. They represented Taiwan, Hong Kong, and the Philippines.

Many other students have been counseled and prayed with, and we know that a beginning has been made toward their meeting the Lord. For some, coming to a retreat may be only one link in the chain of events which the Lord will use to bring them to Himself.

Full of vision and vigorous at eighty-two, Emma, together with helpers, now prepares meals for the student retreats. She plans the menus, shops around to find good bargains as she buys the food, and then oversees the preparation of the meals. She has some special touches as she fixes dishes to appeal to the taste of internationals, such as Wollof rice. But her duties do not end in the kitchen, for she is a full-time assistant to Hanna in other facets of the student ministry and hosts many students and guests in their home.

At Christmas time a general invitation is given out to all students. Those who do not have a place to go for the holidays may come to Fellowship Valley as guests. Some have stayed for a period of weeks, enjoying the warmth of Emma's and Hanna's hospitality and fellowship. Hanna presents a Bible study in the evenings, at which time there is much sharing and fellowshipping. Much spiritual blessing has come to the students as a result of these times of sharing the Word of God.

The monthly student retreats are carefully and prayerfully planned, and invitations are sent out. Hanna seeks the mind of the Lord for the right guest speaker for each retreat. We praise the Lord for the way He draws the students to these weekend gatherings. Some of the students, aware of the racial and national antagonisms between some nations and peoples, are amazed to see the many nationalities eating, living, and having fun together in real harmony. It is a work of the Holy Spirit, we know—a foretaste of heaven.

We never dreamed when we came to Fellowship Valley that the Lord would one day give the retreat an outreach to the ends of the earth! We praise the Lord for the privilege of being co- workers with Him in the world harvest.

One of our earliest international student retreats.

Hanna, fellowshipping with students.

An international student gathering.

A musical presentation from a group of Spanish-speaking students.

What a privilege to minister to students from many countries of the world.

19

The Storm of the Century

On Saturday morning, March 13, 1993, "the storm of the century," as the media named it, was raging through our valley like a midwestern blizzard. Winds were at a gale pitch, driving the snow before them, and boughs on the pine trees sagged under the weight of snow. Temperatures had plunged to an unbelievable low, and the wind chill registered at twenty below zero!! I had never before seen anything like this in Georgia.

In our main meeting room, thirty-seven international students and our staff were holding the first service of the day for the monthly retreat. As I stood looking out at the storm I suddenly realized that we could be in for serious trouble. Snow like this, lying heavily on already sagging limbs of pine trees, could cause extensive power outages. We have suffered such things before. But we have never had thirty-seven people to care for in such a crisis. I say crisis because that is exactly what it becomes. When the power goes out, our lights go out, electrically heated homes are left without heat, the pump for our water ceases to work, which means no water for drinking, cooking, bathing, or toilets. Thermostatically controlled oil heating stoves are of limited use or have to be manually controlled to keep them from overheating.

As the storm rose, I could see that we were in a race against time. We needed to fill pots and barrels with water for cooking, drinking, and bathroom use. I rushed around in the snow, putting barrels into place and then carrying water to them. Staff and guests alike rushed to the modular homes to fill containers there.

Our weekend cooking helper, Ruth Ramey, knowing from experience the dangers of allowing a heavy buildup of snow on the dining room roof, urged Hanna to send some fellows up on the roof with shovels to clear it.

While the storm raged, threatening to topple trees, the students paused in their meeting to pray for the Lord's protection on all of the buildings. Miraculously, the wind died down. Their prayers were heard, for despite reports of heavy damage to buildings from falling trees in cities around us, not one tree fell on any building in our valley. In fact, not one tree fell in the central part of the retreat at all!! Praise His Name!

Most of the students had not come to the retreat prepared for a snowstorm. Many had no boots, gloves, hats, mittens, or warm coats.

After the supper meal and evening meeting were completed, the students went to their rooms for the night. At 9:30

P.M. the electric power went off. We passed out candles for light, but as the hours went by, the rooms became colder and colder. The night was bitterly cold outside, and the chill crept through the walls unrelentingly. We did have propane gas heaters in the dining room which were not dependent upon electricity to operate. But the students decided to remain in their rooms up the hill and bundle up the best they could against the cold. To walk anywhere in the pitch dark night would have been dangerous, for we had had sleet before the snow fell, and footing was treacherous.

Ruth Ramey did manage to make it up the hill to the modular homes with her truck to take a kerosene heating stove to a home where there were two families with children. One couple had a baby only six months old. All were from Africa and not used to a cold climate. We heard the next morning that one father had stayed awake all night holding first one child and then another close to his own body to share some warmth with them, It was a long, difficult night.

The telephone died at the same time the power went off, so the retreat was totally isolated from the outside world. But we were never out of touch with our great Provider, Protector, and Father who controls all things. He kept everyone safe, and in the morning, all the students gathered in the dining room again for breakfast.

Knowing as I did that these power outages can go on for days, I had a fleeting concern about whether we would have enough food to feed all these people if we were snowbound for several days. Georgia so rarely has severe winter weather that the state doesn't own much in the way of snowplows. We usually just sit and wait for the snow to melt. Pondering the possibilities of all this, I decided to contact friends who operate a country inn about one-half mile north of us on our county road. The husband assured me that they were well supplied with food and that we were to let him know if we needed anything. He has a four-wheel-drive jeep which can travel in such weather.

Meanwhile, students were completing their breakfast and Hanna was trying to assess how many were going to attempt to drive their cars up the long, winding road to the ridge of the mountain to get to the highway. She was regaling the students with stories of her adventures in the country of The Gambia during a military coupe. Her tales of God's deliverances and safekeeping in the midst of danger were a faith builder for the students as she encouraged them to trust the Lord in this difficult moment.

Finally, some decided to try for the highway. The rest settled down for a time in the Word together. The guest speaker went with the Chinese students from Clemson University to help them push their cars up the slope if need be. He was gone so long that Hanna had to give a message from the Word extemporaneously. The Chinese students were successful in pushing their cars up to the ridge, and this encouraged others to try. Gradually, the group thinned out as they trudged to their cars and started out of the Valley.

We learned later that a student from Kenya, who had come by car from a place near Asheville, North Carolina, traveled through unbelievable snow and hazardous conditions. He could scarcely tell where he was. He didn't realize until later that officials had discouraged travel in that region, but in the Lord's mercy, he found his way through the snow to his home.

The funny side of the story is that not a half hour after the last student left, a *snowplow* came rushing down into our valley!! It is the first and last one we have ever seen here!

Unfortunately, the power and the telephone did not come back until the following week, after the many trees beyond our valley were lifted from the wires and the service restored. During those days without power, the frigid out-of-doors became our refrigerator, and candles our light.

We thank the Lord for His great protection. We were unscathed, and we know He had His hand upon us all. Damages throughout the southeast region were enormous. It lived up to its name, this "storm of the century!!"

20

Encompassed by Angels

On Palm Sunday afternoon in 1993, at about 3:30 in the afternoon, a massive tornado system roared through Fellowship Valley Retreat. We had tracked it on television as it left seventeen people dead in a church in Piedmont, Alabama. When the tornado warning went into effect in the county next to ours, we went to the basement to take refuge. It was just a matter of minutes before the force of three twisters struck the retreat. They came from several directions, judging by the damage we saw afterward. The main force rushed through from the back forest and left a path of hundreds of torn, broken, and fallen trees as it headed straight for our home. The small metal utility building next to the deck of our house thrashed and crashed as the winds ripped one door off and threw it into the woods behind our house and twisted the second door up over the roof of the shed. When I heard the crashing, I pleaded with the Lord for the safety of our own house. Miraculously, our home stood untouched except for some broken deck furniture and a door panel which was broken by a board that smashed against it. And a glass-topped table on the deck was left unscathed.

Another thrust of the storm swept through in front of the main dining room, pulling trees up by the roots in nearby woods. One large pine crashed down on the roof of the dining room. Another fell on the roof of the dormitory building. A huge white pine was literally "topped" by the storm, and the top section—some twenty feet high—was flung across the driveway near the kitchen and dumped in the ditch.

Driveways were blocked by a maze of fallen trees and snarled electrical wires. Our pickup truck was parked about six feet from the rowboat. A big pine tree was flung down between them, but neither of them was touched! That arm of the storm continued up through the forest toward our new shop and maintenance building, battering trees to the ground along the way. It laid the last trees down just twenty feet short of the building, then jumped *over* the roof of the shop. The terrible devastation continued immediately on the other side of the building and was awful to behold as the storm leveled the trees on our neighbor's property.

Meantime, another twister had branched off from the main part of the storm and had taken a ninety-degree right turn at the top of the ridge, rushing across the county road right through the acres where our four sixty-foot mobile homes sat. Again the destruction was awful. It took down ninety percent of the trees in an area adjacent to the homes. A whole section of forest was gone!! Dozens of trees were downed over the driveway leading to the homes.

After the storm, Alline led me through the debris of twisted, uprooted trees to reach the mobile homes. I cannot describe the feeling I had as we emerged from the woods into the clearing and saw those four homes sitting there UNHARMED in that gray, unnaturally quiet and darkly overcast aftermath of the storm. It was amazing and wonderful!! One big sixty-foot pine had crashed to the ground full length parallel to one of the homes but had not touched it. Another large pine had fallen onto the roof of another home, but its sturdy heavy limbs had served as shock absorbers and had caused the weight of the trunk to bounce, leaving the roof undamaged! It was unbelievable. Mobile homes do not simply SIT STILL as a tornado roars through their midst!! They explode and blow

Twenty-five trees were blown down over one driveway.

away!! It had to be the Lord's angels who stood there to protect them.

And there were more angels obviously at work. A third twister had roared in from another direction in our back woods and rushed straight cross the lake past three cabins, laying down trees by the cabins as it went. One particular tree would surely have crushed one of the cabins had it not been for the new deck we had just installed on the side of the cabin about two days before. The deck railing caught the weight of the tree and kept it from smashing down on the cabin roof.

As this tornado roared across the lake and felled trees across the county road, it headed straight for Hanna's and Em's double-wide mobile home. The storm pushed trees over on its way up their driveway. Then, just twenty feet from the front deck it suddenly jumped right over the house, flipping off the metal fireplace chimney as it went. The twister came down immediately at the edge of the rear deck of the house and smashed the trees there. *More* angels watched over this home, we are sure of that!! There can be no doubt that the *Lord* kept the tornadoes from demolishing our homes and buildings!

We noted another unusual touch of the Lord's hand when we saw that one tornado had swept through the front yard of our main dining building near the campfire circle. We normally have dozens of plastic, lawn chairs sitting in a horseshoe shape around the fire circle. When the winds hit this area, it scattered the chairs like straws in a gale. All but one! One chair remained just where it had been all through the storm. We were touched when we saw what was sitting in the seat of that chair—a small, white, stuffed lamb. It had been left there by a little girl the week before. We thought it was a lovely picture of how the Lord had protected us and the retreat when other things were being blown away.

Another startling story emerged from the storm. We usually have a large work team of teens and adults come from my home church in Minneapolis during the Easter break. They have been coming for years to help us with projects. But this particular year—1993—I had a strong feeling that we should tell them not to come. I thought perhaps it was because we didn't have funds to carry out the projects they needed to do. I wrote in February to tell them not to come. If they *had* come, they would have arrived at the *very hour* the tornadoes hit our valley! Praise the Lord for His mercy in sharing His foreknowledge with us, preventing a possible tragedy. We have no basements big enough to house such a large group of people to keep them safe.

We had just concluded a week of wonderful accomplishments with a work team from Florida the day before the tornadoes came. The men had returned to their homes in Florida on Saturday. About one-and-a-half hours after the storm hit us on Sunday afternoon, I called Bob Flack in Seminole, Florida. "I'm glad you arrived home safely, Bob," I said. "Would you like to come back?" After hearing the extent of the damages we suffered, he called another friend and they *did* come back the next day. They stayed for another week, helping to remove trees from the power lines and the driveways. They moved large pines from the dining room and dormitory roofs and repaired the damage. We were without lights, water, and heat for forty-seven hours. County emergency services and a friend brought water to us.

It is estimated that we lost four or five hundred trees on the retreat property. Our nature trails were obliterated, covered over with fallen trees and limbs. In addition to the trees already down, others were leaning dangerously and needed to be cut down. Months after the storm, trees were still falling down.

Things could have been much worse. Just a few miles across country from us, an elderly lady was killed by the storm. Many chicken farmers lost their entire chicken barns with thousands of chickens inside. Our property was festooned with bits of yellow insulation blown here from chicken barns destroyed many miles away. Some people north of us were hit with hail the size of baseballs. Others lost their homes or their roofs. News sources reported that the path of the tornado system was between one-fourth and one-half mile wide as it traveled the entire width of the state of Georgia from Alabama. We can only give thanks to God for His great mercy toward us. It is obvious that He stationed angels here in the valley to keep us and our buildings safe.

A large international student retreat was scheduled for the weekend just five days after the tornado. Driveways were buried under fallen trees. We had no water or electricity. Nevertheless, Hanna determined that should the Lord see fit to clear the driveways so that we could get around the grounds the retreat would be held!! Sure enough, the Lord did bring enough help to clear the driveways, and the power lines were repaired in time to restore us to operation. Volunteers even came from Florida to assist Emma with the cooking that weekend.

When we brought in machinery to help clear the multitude of fallen trees in the central part of the retreat, we piled up the trees to see if we could sell them to a lumber mill. Our helpers had cut them to mill lengths. Our piles were immense! We soon had a *log yard!!* We called a man who owns a small lumber mill, and he took many of the logs away to make rough lumber for us. The pile of fine boards was stacked for drying, so then we had a *lumber* yard! We began to use the boards for building projects. The eighteen-foot 2'x6's made fine joists for a storage building and beams for roof projects! So it, indeed, became a case of beauty from ashes!

The Lord never wastes any of our experiences. They always have some good purpose in His plan for us. Our part is to take the difficulty and carefully watch in faith to see what He is trying to say to us or teach us through it. We have seen His wonderful power demonstrated on our behalf in the face of a storm which could have completely wiped out the retreat facilities. We know that God's protective hand was upon us and that His angels were all around us.

21

Deluges!!

First, it was tornadoes, then came the *floods!!* We had never seen anything like the deluge of rain which fell on our area for nearly two months in 1994. In one twenty-four-hour period, we had thirteen inches of rain! As the flood of water flowed down from the mountains, it took its normal course and ran down to the flat areas of Atlanta, Macon, and on to Albany. Unprecedented floodwaters swept into Macon, and then to cities along the Flint and Chattahoochee Rivers farther south. Alline's brother, Charlie, was Director of Chehaw Park in Albany. He worked desperately to rescue the many exotic animals in his care. It was reported that two young bears stood on tiptoe for twenty-four hours to keep their noses above water until they could be rescued.

The storms were the result of two tropical depressions which swept north out of the Gulf of Mexico with a hurricane-like movement, bringing their torrential rains far north as the system swirled. It moved back to the Gulf to gather more moisture and then surged again to the north. The first depression, Alberto, stalled over Georgia, delivered heavy rains, and caused the rivers to swell as they headed south. We in the mountains suffered no real damage from this first storm, but devastation was in the making for the cities to the south. When the *second* tropical depression moved in just a short time later, we began to see things here that we had never witnessed before. Overnight, the tremendous deluge of rain brought our two lakes to the overflow level. We had a white-water river rushing torrentially in several directions down from the emergency spillway of our earthen dam at the main lake. The lake level was only about thirty inches below the top of the dam itself. Some of the overflow was rushing toward the county road. The rest was rolling down the hillside to smash against the side of our mill with its water wheel. The high-water mark on the side of that building one morning was about forty inches. For the first time, the lake flooded up into the campfire circle area in front of the main dining room. It also covered the path along the edge of the lake. The situation looked so dangerous for our earthen dam that I rushed to the house to call the Soil Conservation Department. They came to check it immediately. One of the men said to me, "It will be all right if we don't get too much more rain." Great comfort that was in the face of the heavy gray clouds which continued to unload heavy rains on us for days to come. But we praise the Lord that the dam held!

    The county road superintendent arrived to survey the damage the heavy runoff had done to the county road which runs past our front gate. His recommendations for correcting the runoff for the future would have been very expensive. Trying to stop the velocity of rushing waters as they come down hillsides onto the driveways and roads is a daunting challenge at best. Our own driveways were a terrible mess from the storm. What could we possibly do to correct the problem?

    After the road superintendent left, I drove into town on business. When I returned, I couldn't believe my eyes! A miraculous transformation had occurred in my absence! Our driveways were completely made over! Not only were they professionally graded, but they were freshly *graveled!* And there, standing on the corner of our front entrance was the man we consider to be the finest grader operator in the county, Hayward Bryson. He was waiting for the arrival of another load

Deluges!!

of gravel to finish the job on our drive. The road superintendent had sent him out to the retreat to assess our road problems and see what could be done to fix it. He had FIXED it all right!! Using his fine grader he had redone the driveway in an expert way. Then he used special grading techniques to redirect the runoff in the future so that it will go into the existing drains and culvert rather than run all over the road. How we thank the Lord for this amazing solution to our urgent need. The Lord surely does the impossible! "He moves in a mysterious way, His wonders to perform!!"

22

The Lord's Unique Building Plan

Our beautiful retreat property has no open, level space where we can build the big conference center which we had envisioned for so long. The forest is close in around us. So we looked in faith for additional acres. In the woods at the south edge of our property lay a piece of land which we felt might lend itself to our building need. It was owned by a Christian couple whom we knew. We had prayed about this land, but we had no money with which to buy it.

Then suddenly in 1997, in a most unexpected manner, the Lord began to open the way toward the future building program. During the Christmas holidays, He sent us several large gifts of money which were not designated for any particular phase of our ministry.

I had just been reading in the Old Testament of how the Lord opened the waters before His people so they could pass through the Red Sea. It encouraged my heart. I said to Alline, "We have been sitting on 'square one' for so long concerning the building program and the land we need to buy for the erection of the lodge. Let's take these funds and *move ahead*." The money we had on hand was *not* enough to pay for the land, but perhaps we could arrange a long- term contract with the owner, if need be. Let's just *move ahead!* Alline agreed, "Let's do it!" So we called the men on our Board of Trustees. They rose to the challenge, too! Soon afterward Alline came back to my house and said, "I forgot, we *do* have several major financial commitments to handle in the next few months." I groaned inside, not wanting to turn back. After she left I said to the Lord, "PLEASE Lord, do SOMETHING to get us over this hump!" The next day we received a gift of $10,000! And a very short time later He sent us $5,000 more! The house *really* rang with praise! Then we received a gift of *$25,000!* There was no question about moving ahead. He had given us marching orders, loud and clear!

So, with money in hand to pay CASH for the five acres, another staff lady and I went to see Mr. & Mrs. Harry Hilliard, the owners.

But the Lord had yet another surprise for us. As we chatted with the Hilliards, he told us that they had decided to GIVE us the land! We returned home on "cloud nine," rejoicing in the Lord!

In the early part of this story we told you about a man who came to us in the days following our discovery of the Fellowship Valley property. He is Tom Gregory, a very fine architect and also a Christian brother. He has stood with us for over twenty years, waiting for the Lord's time to build. Through this long period, he and his team of architectural craftsmen have done much to encourage and help us along the way.

We are excited by the plans he has produced for a two-story lodge and conference center. The middle section of the building will consist of a conference room upstairs to seat 150 and a dining room downstairs for 150, as well as two small seminar rooms. In the basement there will be a large seminar room and offices. Extending out from each side of the conference section will be wings of sleeping quarters with enough space for sixty people. It nearly took our breath away when Tom gave us his estimate for the cost of this conference center—*One and a half million dollars!* There is no doubt that we face a mountain of impossibility! But the Lord said that if we have faith as a grain of mustard seed we *can say* to this mountain—"be thou removed, and it will be removed!" With God *nothing* is impossible.

The Lord has His own ways of preparing us for the BIG leaps of faith. Often He starts with *smaller* steps, which teach us to depend on Him and strengthen us for the "mountain-moving" tasks ahead.

We take steps of faith when the Lord says "Come!" and invites us to walk on the water with Him. We know that the moment we obey and step over the side of the boat we are leaving behind all security. We are entering a realm where God must display His supernatural power or we will sink. But in many situations we have seen that it *delights* the Lord to show His power, as long as it brings glory to His Name. He didn't open the Red Sea to give Moses a reputation as a great man of faith. Neither will He show His power to make *us* a name! *He* must have all the credit and the glory.

Timing is all important! Even when the Lord tells us what He is going to do, He may not plan to carry it through right away. And it is at this juncture where we so often get into difficulty. God has His own timetable and nothing will change that. He told Joseph through several dreams what He planned to do. But soon afterward Joseph found himself caught up in a series of painful, unexpected circumstances which changed his life. He was thrown into a pit, sold into slavery, taken to a foreign land, falsely accused, and imprisoned! And there he waited, *until the Lord's time came.* Psalm 105:18–19 tells of his dilemma: "Whose feet they hurt with fetters: he was laid in iron: *Until the time that his word came: The word of the Lord tried him.*" Joseph knew God intended to place him in an exalted position. The dreams had foretold that. As he sat in prison, he must have wondered what had gone wrong. Of course he had his battles. It *says* that the *word of the Lord tried him*. He was being tested. His faith in God's stated plan for him was being refined. He thought that perhaps Pharaoh's chief butler was going to get him released. But it did not happen. It was not yet God's *time*. And so the refining and strengthening process continued.

In like manner, having given us His plan for the Valley, the Lord put a comma, as it were, and gave us a waiting time. And what an *exciting* time it has been!

Alline was out walking one morning when she noticed a man standing beside the road looking at one of our signs. He asked her if she could tell him anything about this place. So she began describing the ministry of Fellowship Valley. Then she said, "If you are really interested in learning more, come over to my house and I will give you a book which tells all about it." Jack Horne took the book with him to Glen-Ella Springs Hotel, a nearby country inn, where he and his wife, Marie, were celebrating their fortieth wedding anniversary. The next morning he returned with his wife. They had read the book and were keenly interested in becoming involved! We gave them a tour of the grounds and buildings. As we strolled along the lake, we passed an open space near our long, arched bridge. I commented that someday we hoped to have a nice gazebo there. It was a beautiful spot where future retreat guests using the gazebo could read, pray, have fellowship, or just be quiet.

Jack and Marie returned to their home in South Carolina. About a week later he called us and said, "We would like to build that gazebo for you!" At that time we learned that he was an engineer. In the spring he gathered a team of helpers who came to build a beautiful gazebo. As they were completing work on it, we had a phone call from Charles Cornelius of Valdosta, Georgia. We didn't know him at all, but he had read the first edition of our book. He is a landscaper, and he just wondered if we could use any help with *landscaping!* God's perfect timing! We had planned on a garden of perennials, such as azaleas, below the gazebo. Charles came the following week with his pickup truck loaded with plants and stayed several days to use his skills to beautify different areas of the grounds.

Wayne Prosser, a member of our Advisory Board and a missionary builder with Ambassadors For Christ International, took Fellowship Valley "under his wing" as a special project. He came and put a new roof on several buildings, built a fine deck, and did some excellent remodeling and repair for us. He and his wife, Joan, along with other helpers, teamed up in these efforts.

On one occasion Wayne and a work crew came to re-roof a cabin and add a 16' by 16' addition. One of the volunteer carpenters on this job, Moe Starling, slipped from the rafters and fell headfirst to the floor below. He narrowly missed striking his head on the concrete. We quickly called 911 as Wayne and Harold Carlson, another worker, prayed over Moe. We thanked the Lord that Moe's injuries, a broken collar bone and a separated shoulder, though serious and long lasting, were not life threatening.

It was only weeks later in 1998 that Wayne suffered a tragic accident which nearly took his life. While working on an apartment building in Missouri, he, his son Matthew, and nephew John had to set up a long aluminum ladder against a building. Matthew began to climb the ladder when a high-voltage power line unexpectedly arced to the top of the ladder and sent powerful surges of electricity through him. His legs were set on fire. Wayne and John both rushed to his aid. They grabbed the ladder to pull Matthew away. Immediately, *they* were electrocuted and thrown to the ground by the force of the high voltage.

It "just so happened" that a very fine EMC man was there in the apartment complex and he hurried to help them. All three men were taken to the hospital emergency room. Matthew and John both suffered serious injury and Wayne's life hung by a thread, *God's thread,* for a long time. He was in a coma and given little or no chance of survival. After many weeks his doctor said to Wayne's wife, "take him wherever he is going to be buried." The Prossers are Canadians and Joan decided on further treatment in New Brunswick. Her long bedside vigil has been a true test of faith. At the time of this writing (2001), Wayne has definitely shown some improvement, but still cannot talk or use his limbs properly. He is somewhat like a stroke victim now, recognizing various people and trying to make sounds. What a triumph it would be—and a glory to the Lord's name—to see Wayne whole again! We would love to have him with us for the construction of the conference center! With *God,* all things are possible.

The next step in the *Lord's* building program was a real surprise! We received a letter from a young man who had been constructing log homes for some time. He was now going out of business and wondered whether we would be interested in some leftover logs and roof trusses he had stored in his barn. The value would be about $20,000.

We were really excited by the possibility of using our available funds along with his lumber supplies to do a project. We had prayed so long for new buildings and this looked like an answer from the Lord. Our board considered this offer and decided we should go ahead. Our architect, Tom Gregory, did the final drawings and we were launched! We had designed a plan for a two-story log building with a meeting room downstairs and retreat guest bedrooms upstairs. It was in the fall of 1998 when our lumber donor, Randy Frost, decided to be the contractor for the job and started the excavation work.

We had just gotten underway when we received word from Dick and Mavis Linder that the Lord had called them to join our staff. We had been praying for them and had corresponded with them for several years about coming. But their answer had been negative up until then. This was the couple I envisioned as the new leaders of the ministry. Dick and Mavis had served in Canada among Eskimos for seven years before going to Brazil, where they spent thirty-four years. Dick had been the pastor of one of the churches founded by their ministry. He was also a teacher in the Bible school their mission had established. Even though they were with a work in Brazil, it had been in my heart and prayers for several years that the Lord would have Dick take up the directorship from Alline and me when that time came.

In recent years, their mission had turned over the work in Brazil to the Brazilians who had been trained under their leadership. The Linders came home to the States in 1998. They had completed arrangements to retire to Bradenton Missionary Village in Florida when the Lord interrupted their plans with a surprising one of His own! He spoke to them about laying aside their retirement to join our staff, which they did. In February of 2000 Dick was installed as the new director of Fellowship Valley (Faith Ventures, Inc.).

In the months prior to the Linders' coming, we had added a new staff worker, Marilyn Rose. She had read our Fellowship Valley story, *Two Weak Women and Amazing Grace*, at her home in Illinois. She felt led of the Lord to come and help in the work here. For years her personal ministry had been to give out good Christian books to people in need. In obedience to the Lord she sold her home, parted with many of her possessions, and stepped out by faith to serve the Lord. She has served faithfully and well, using her skills in the job of head bookkeeper. She has also carried on some book distribution. More recently she has felt that the Lord is leading her to another ministry in a nearby location. We will greatly miss her fellowship and her willing, servant spirit.

When we heard that the Linders were coming, we knew that the Lord had meant this log building for *staff housing* rather than for meeting and guest space. We quickly re-drew the plans, laid out a two-story, two-family house, and Randy moved on with the bulldozing!

Building the log home was an education in itself. It was also another wonderful display of the Lord's power to provide. Subcontractors came and went with regularity. A number of them gave discounts or made cash gifts to the work of Fellowship Valley. Along with these, a $5,000 gift came and then three of $1,000 each. Dee Hurm, an electrician from Florida, arrived to wire the house. He was assisted by George Watson of Helen, Georgia. Five young men drove down from Minnesota to help put up roof trusses and sheeting, and to do other needed jobs. Several men came from within Georgia to raise walls and do interior framing or finishing work.

Other encouragements came at this time—a well-kept Oldsmobile car and a handsome golf cart (one of our chief work vehicles) arrived.

As we came to the furnishing of the new home, we saw wonderful answers to prayer.

First we needed kitchen cabinets for the upstairs apartment. Knowing that these were going to be expensive, we decided to ask a Christian woodworker for counsel on where to obtain cabinets. When we talked to our friend, Johnny Whiting, he said, "I've read your book and I would like to do something for your work!" He proceeded to obtain and then install a beautiful set of oak cabinets. To complete the job he even added one of those fine pantry units with revolving shelves! It was all a *gift!* Even the counter tops were a marvel! A friend from Du Pont Co. offered us CORION material for the counters. And it was installed without charge! We have never had such elegant counters before. There is no end to the Lord's wonderful works.

Then we needed a stove, fridge, and dishwasher. Our friend, Bill Junkin, has been coming for a retreat with a singles' group for several years. His regular job is installing appliances.

The Lord's Unique Building Plan

He and his family and his employer teamed up to supply a fridge and gas stove. Bill gave the dishwasher. Then other friends said, "Oh, we have a new hood you can have for the stove and a microwave oven!"

Next the man came from the gas company to hook up the cooking stove. As we stood there watching he turned to us and asked, "What about the stove downstairs?"

"We don't have one yet," I replied.

"Well, we are going to *give* you one," he said. What a wonderful surprise! The *gas* company was going to give us a new gas range! And they *did!*

Dick and Mavis moved into their new home. Within weeks, Dick suffered a heart attack and had heart bypass work done. The Lord worked graciously and he is fine now.

Dick Linder baptizing a student
who was saved during a retreat.

Proposed Chalet & Conference Center

Present Modular Homes

Staff Home

Present dir
meeting ro

Fellov
Lak

sent dorm

Cabin

Three Cabins

Maintenance Bldg.

Staff Home

Mill

Staff Home

Bonnie Hanson and architect Tom Gregory checking the Lodge plans at the site.

Alline Marshall looks on as Harry Hilliard signs the deed for five acres over to Fellowship Valley.

The proposed Lodge/conference center.

- The new chalet/conference lodge will be constructed of cedar and stone.
- It will contain 20 bedrooms which will care for 60 people, but additional sleeping space can be arranged to accommodate about six more.
- The various wings of sleeping units are designed for use by either large or small groups and can be heated or cooled according to need.

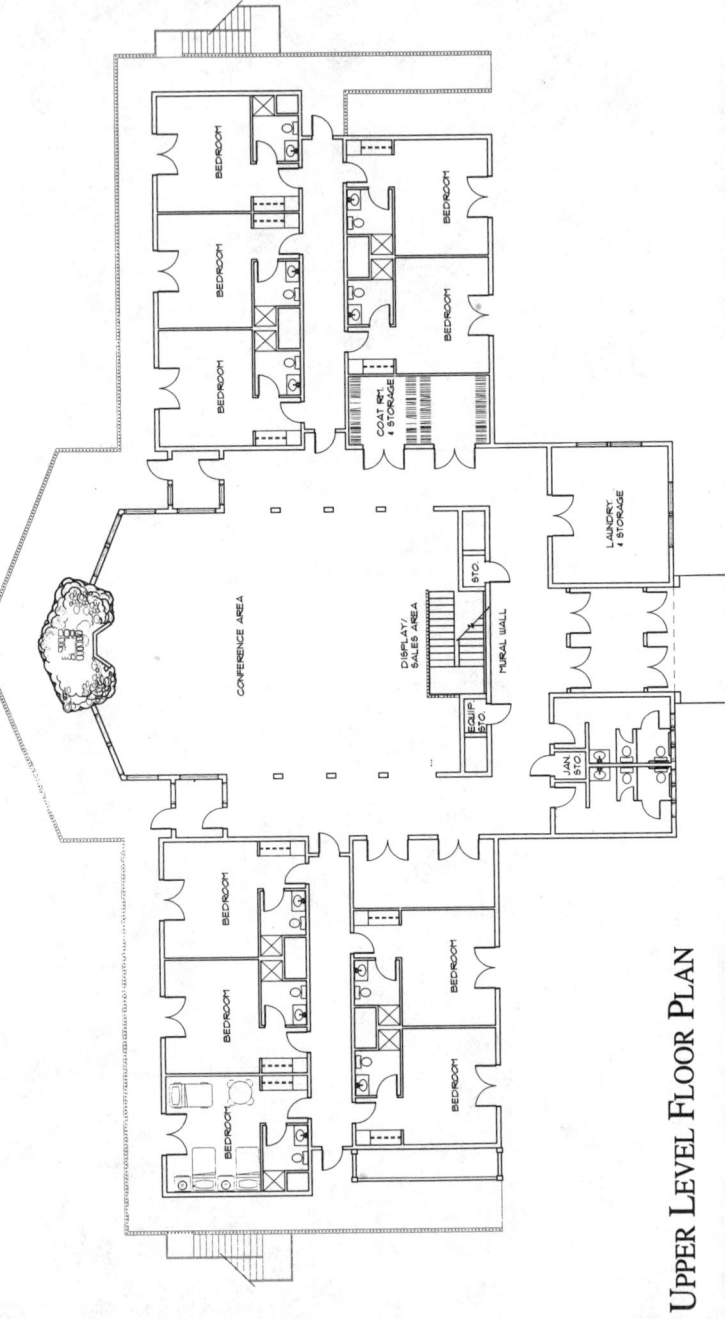

UPPER LEVEL FLOOR PLAN

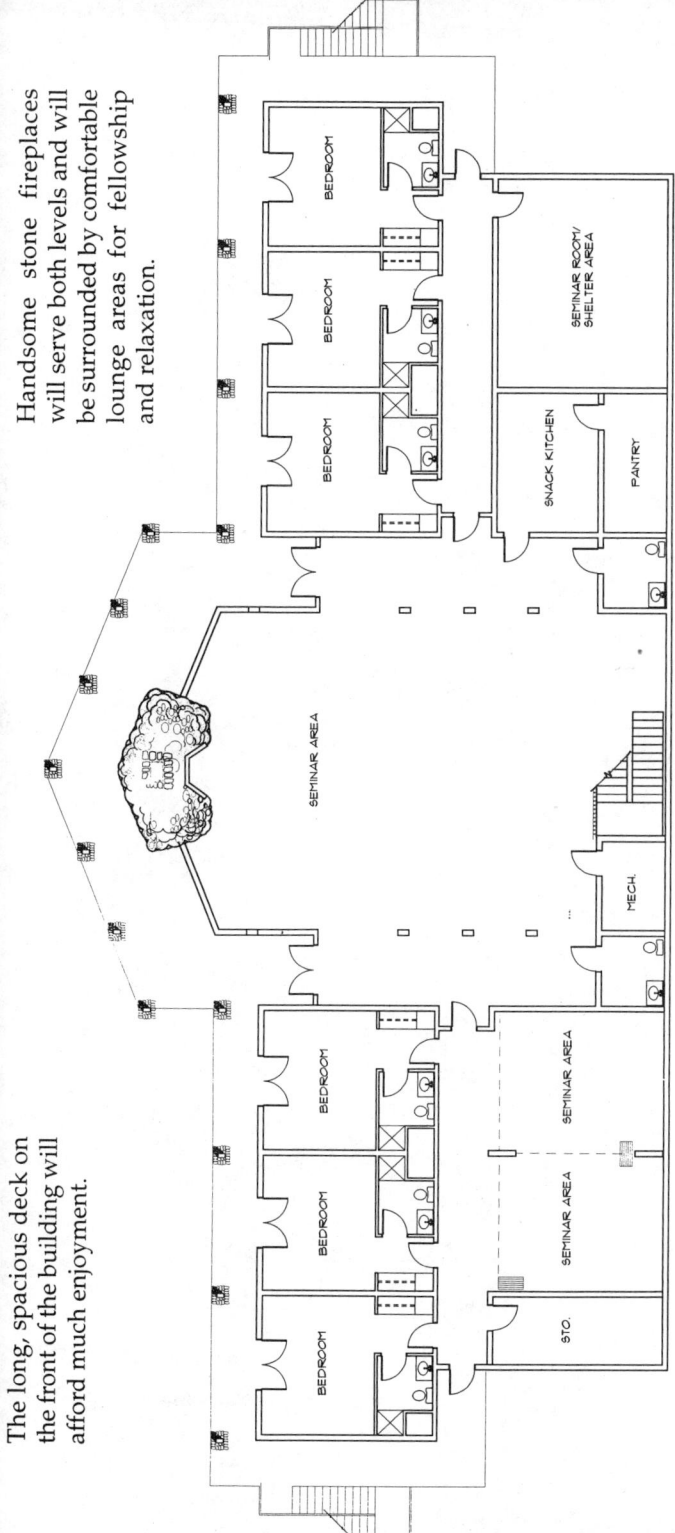

23

The Fingerprints of God

It was a beautiful morning and I was settling down to some sign lettering in my home when a pickup truck parked in front of the house. I stepped out on the front deck to see who it might be, and found myself at the beginning of a new set of God's miracles!! The couple who came up to my living room had found our book, *Two Weak Women and Amazing Grace,* in a store just two days before. They read it and came to the mountains to find us! Deborah, the wife, said to me, "This is no accident. We believe that the Lord wants us to help you." They said that as they read the book they saw that we needed to build new facilities . . . and they own a construction company!!! God had impressed their hearts with a burden to assist us with that task.

As I took them on a walking tour of the grounds and buildings, we talked of various needs. They made mental notes, obviously, for Deborah called me in the next several days to say that they would like to bring a crew of volunteers to tear down one of the old, deteriorated cabins on the lakeshore and then build a new one in its place. Great joy filled my heart as the Lord brought this couple alongside to encourage us. We had been praying for many years for the beginning of new buildings to replace our old ones. The summer camp facilities we inherited with the property are in a sad state of decay, and it is URGENT for us to put new ones in place if our ministry is to continue. One of the wonders of this contact with Deborah and Glynn Galloway is that they have known our architect, Tom Gregory, for years. So they will be working with him as we move along. The lakeside cabin project began on August 19, 2000, when the Galloways brought their team of helpers and tore down the old cabin. After lunch that day a white SUV drove into the retreat and parked in front of my house. Alline and I walked down to see who this might be. It was Calvin and Pat Bryan. They had found our book in a Christian bookstore, read it, and had come to find us. Pat said, "This is no accident." They, too, sensed that the Lord was in our meeting together. We learned that Calvin is in charge of electrical matters for a suburb near Atlanta. He strolled over to our builder friend, Glynn Galloway, and said to him, "When you get this cabin built, call me and I will come and wire it for you!!"

The weekend after we met Glynn and Deborah, Alline and I drove to Knoxville, Tennessee, to see Joan, the wife of Wayne Prosser, who was electrocuted. While we were there, our board member, Jeff Brooks, gave me a new computer. As Alline and I rode along on our way home that afternoon, I remarked, "We need to get a fax machine." The next day Deborah and Glynn came to see us, and what do you suppose they brought for the ministry . . . a FAX MACHINE!!

We hired Steve Newsome, a local backhoe man, to excavate the basement for the cabin. Then another special blessing of the Lord arrived. Joe Vara, a sub-contractor in concrete work, volunteered his machinery, his crew, time and skills, to put in forms and do the basement. Glynn then brought several carpenter friends to help him frame in the downstairs of the house. What a blessing to watch the Lord build the building as He brought skilled, willing helpers to the job!

Through the weeks, we saw more gracious carpenters donating long hours and strength to bring this cabin from stage to stage. Glynn's twin brother, Lynn, as well as another brother, Jerry, have both done a lot. And the wives have worked right along with their husbands, carrying lumber, measuring boards, using the big saw, etc.

As we walked in faith, trusting the Lord for the needs, He sent financial gifts. One dear couple donated funds to cover the floor and roof trusses. They also paid the plumber who did the rough plumbing under the basement floor. We received a gift of $500 from a man who read our Fellowship Valley story and enjoyed it very much. Another $500 came from a church whose young people had been here earlier in the year for a mission-training time. We walk "on the waters" as it were, trusting the Lord for His provision, and He is truly faithful.

As we neared the time when we would install the heating and air conditioning equipment, a company owned by fine Christian friends donated all the heating and air conditioning equipment and supplies!! The next miracle on the list was to see the Lord provide a skilled man to install these systems. We also needed a plumber to do the remaining plumbing. Enter Tom Slagle, a licensed plumber and heating and air conditioning man. He had sold his business to go into full-time service for the Lord. He had some time free and went right to work on the project!! Isn't the lord wonderful?!!

After Tom Slagle sold his business, he had a warehouse well-stocked with repair parts for plumbing, heating and electrical work. He invited us to bring a truck and load it up with whatever we could use. In addition he gave a table saw, a Roto Rooter machine, and other equipment. What a tremendous and generous gift this was to us!! And what about the floor covering in the cabin?? The Lord has that in hand, too. A kind gentleman who has a carpeting business has promised us all the carpeting we will need for this new building.

Long ago the Lord began to supply some of the furnishings for the cabin. We have a huge pile of twin beds stacked neatly all the way to the rafters in our big maintenance shop, just waiting for the big day of moving in!! We were also given a washer and dryer for the laundry where the sheets for this cabin will be washed when a retreat group leaves. We also have a good supply of bedspreads and some of the lamps for bedrooms. More recently, the Lord put it into the heart of Bonnie's cousin, June, to send sets of sheets for each of those beds, plus enough towels and wash cloths for use in the cabin!

Friends in Canada called to ask if we needed any help with landscaping on our grounds. That was timely, for we will be needing beautification around the new cabin. We thank the Lord for bringing help for each need. It is clear that HE is in the constructing of the buildings here at Fellowship Valley!!

During these exciting weeks while the cabin was progressing, we had a call from a friend who comes with a women's retreat group each October. She asked if we could use an ice-making machine. We exclaimed, "YES!" We have needed one for many years! She told us that her church wanted to give us one! Praise the Lord!

Chuck Smith, a Christian brother whose business is the installation of ice machines, was hired by the church for this job. Chuck was also given a copy of our book to read and was blessed. He has since become a friend of the ministry and will service the new ice maker twice a year without charge!

In August, the Lord sent a friend who could wire our new office for the telephones we needed for the fax machine and the computers. He arrived just as we needed this job done. The Lord's timing is perfect!!

The Lord continued to put in place His chosen workers to strengthen the staff. In the summer of 1999, Gary and Shari Hedwall, who had worked with Dick and Mavis Linder in Brazil, came to visit the Valley. The Hedwalls had settled in Tennessee, where they had retired and built their dream home. As they traveled back to Tennessee, the Lord surprised them with the thought of returning to His service . . . at Fellowship Valley!! The had long since considered themselves past the point

The Fingerprints of God

in their lives that they would be involved in such a launch of faith. What about support? How would that be met at their age and stage of life?!! And what about their home?!! And what would their daughter say? She had just come to Tennessee to settle close to them. These were big questions. They decided to pray about the matter, and they put several "fleeces" before the Lord. If he met these, then it would be a sure indication that He was in such a step.

They returned to Fellowship Valley later that summer to attend the twentieth anniversary of the ministry. One of their fleeces concerned their support. They said, "Lord, if this is of you, then have someone say to us that they will be one of our supporters." Amazingly enough, the couple who shared the same house they stayed in, said to them, "If you are really serious about this step of serving the Lord here, we would like to be your first supporters!!!" It was a joyous moment of praise. The second "fleece" concerned the sale of their home . . . their dream home! The Lord brought a buyer who was just right for the home! The third "fleece" was also answered speedily. Gary and Shari came and settled into their new responsibilities and have become valuable members of the team. Gary manages the maintenance of the facilities and grounds. He also serves on the development committee and uses his gifts and skills in carpentry and building to assist with construction. He is a tremendous gift to the work. Shari is now the bookkeeper for the ministry as well as assisting with catering of meals for the international student retreats. Gary also takes part in the student work. How we thank the Lord for this excellent couple who were willing and obedient in laying aside retirement and their dream home to answer the Lord's call to active service again.

Life is never dull here at Fellowship Valley, especially when Alline is involved. One afternoon she volunteered to do some lawn mowing, since there was a shortage of manpower at the time. She had already done most of the grounds and was just finishing the area around our earthen dam. She told me that she had just a little more to do. As I was sitting in my living room I suddenly felt led to pray for her safety. About thirty minutes later she walked into my house dripping wet from head to toe!! She was on the dam making a sharp turn when the rider mower began to slip downhill toward the lake. Helpless to stop it, she found herself plunging into the water along with the mower, and then sinking. She was able to extricate her legs from under the mower and climb out of the lake. She was bruised from the fall, but otherwise unhurt . . . except for her dignity!!

We began to feel we were having an epidemic of these wild adventures when the next event took place. Gary, our new maintenance and grounds manager, was using a very heavy hand-guided trenching machine one morning. He was putting in erosion-control silt fences on the embankment below the lakeside building site. Suddenly the machine hung up on tree roots, bucked as it fought the entanglement, overturned, and flung Gary bodily into the lake. In the Lord's mercy, the trencher stopped its plunge and lay on its side near the water. Gary emerged soaked, muddy, and not a little embarrassed.

We are convinced that the Lord has a great sense of humor. Just as Alline's 1987 Olds with 249,000 miles on it was "dying," some friends asked if anyone at the retreat needed a car. "Yes, we need one," I replied. Little did I ever dream that the new car could be a beautiful Lincoln Town Car!! Realizing that some people might wonder at a poor missionary worker driving around in such a posh car, she thought of a solution. She should perhaps have me make a sign to put on the back of the car, saying, "Now faith is the substance of things hoped for . . . !"

Our faithful elderly trucks are in great need of replacement. A young woman near Augusta, Georgia, read our book and noted the way in which the Lord supplied vehicles for us. She and her husband had a Chevy S–10 sitting in their yard. It was no longer needed because they now had a new truck. So they gave the Chevy to us!! It is a fine truck and is giving us very good service. We thank the Lord for it.

We have realized that the development of the ministry and the amount of work there is to be done here at the Valley calls for more staff. We have prayed much for new workers. In early 2001 the Lord sent Steve and Sonia Cowart and their two sons, Stephen and Joshua. This excellent couple are already training into some phases of the international student work along with other responsibilities. They each bring special skills, gifts and experience which can be greatly used in the work here. Steve is also an ordained minister.

Tree surgeon, Mark DeFoor, gave his services to remove tall pines from the building site.

Gary and Shari Hedwall

Joe Vara and crew set up concrete forms for basement of new cabin.

Steve and Sonia Cowart and their sons, Stephen and Joshua.

Dick and Mavis Linder

A time of worship in a women's retreat for the Daughters of the King.

Steve Cowart with an Armenian mother and her two daughters. All three came to the Lord at international student retreat meetings.

Mrs. Marilyn Rose

Glynn and Deborah Galloway, who came to help us build.

Pat and Calvin Bryan, who came after reading our book. Calvin wired the new cabin.

Part of a team from South Carolina doing an excellent paint job.

Alline and Bonnie with the fine team of volunteers who dismantled the lakeside cabin.

24

Lord, Give Us This Mountain!!

This is the beginning of the greatest challenge we have ever faced! In the early pages of this story we told you about our reaction when we first stood on the Fellowship Valley property. The Lord lifted our eyes so that we did not see the debris! We saw only the POTENTIAL! We have worked hard toward realizing that goal of our potential, but we have not achieved it yet.

One afternoon in 1979, our first year in the Valley, I overheard a conversation between a father and his son who were cleaning up after a day of volunteer work. The twelve-year-old boy said to his father, "Dad, do you think this place will ever amount to anything?" His question startled me, but I could see why he wondered about it. The grounds were in an overgrown, cluttered state and the buildings were decaying so that the retreat didn't seem to have much future, except to those with eyes of faith!!

We serve One who always sees the potential in people and situations. He saw the possibilities in some rough fishermen who by His power became flaming evangelists to the world. And He saw the potential in five loaves and three fishes as a means of feeding the multitude. He still has the power to take weak people and make them into instruments that he can use for His purposes. This is the great God we serve!

Two Weak Women

In the 1950's, when I was a young candidate for service with Christian Literature Crusade (the foreign mission Alline and I served with), the Lord impressed on my heart the challenges and promises of Isaiah 58. Now, more than forty years later, I see that the truth and the outworking of these words were meant for the work here in the Retreat. I will quote only a portion of this chapter which especially relates to our present work.

> Is not this the fast that I have chosen? to loose the bands of wickedness, to undo the heavy burdens, and to let the oppressed go free, and that ye break every yoke? Is it not to deal thy bread to the hungry, and that thou bring the poor that are cast out to thy house? when thou seest the naked, that thou cover him; and that thou hide not thyself from thy own flesh? ... And if thou draw out thy soul to the hungry, and satisfy the afflicted soul; then shall thy light rise in obscurity, and thy darkness be as the noon day: And the Lord shall guide thee continually, and satisfy thy soul in drought, ... and thou shalt be like a watered garden, and like a spring of water, whose waters fail not.

This is the ministry which is going on now and will continue at Fellowship Valley—a reaching out and drawing in of lives which are bound, hurting, oppressed, and broken. It is a ministry of praying, counseling, teaching, encouraging, and deepening in Christ.

We have seen so many with broken hearts, people weeping and praying and finding help as those near them gather around them to pray. We have seen men and women released from the power of sin and darkness, bonds broken by the power of Christ. We have had men's groups before the Lord in worship and prayer, spending time in His Word as they meet with Him. Young people have come and discovered that there is relief from the pressures and struggles they face—an answer to be found in Christ! Men and women with troubled marriages have found help and reconciliation through counseling and prayer. We take no credit for what is happening here. We are merely the Lord's servants and His channels. We rejoice and praise Him and give Him all the glory for what has been accomplished. He deliberately "chooses the weak things, the foolish things, so that no flesh shall glory in His presence."

We have marveled as we have received young men and women from over seventy nations of the world, coming to hear the Word of God. One Thanksgiving evening, Hanna's home was packed with thirty Chinese watching the Jesus film in Mandarin. My living room was filled with Russian Jews, seeing the Jesus film in the Russian language. It was probably the first time they had heard the story of Christ and His life laid down for their redemption.

Then there was the weekend when the Valley was filled with the excited, joyous fellowship of Japanese students on retreat. Three gave their hearts to Christ.

A card-carrying Communist from mainland China came to a student retreat with his wife. He spoke no English, but watched the Jesus film in Chinese. She accepted the Lord that evening, but he said he could not become a Christian because he was a Communist. He was apparently concerned about the persecution he would face in China if he became a Christian. When he and his wife returned to South Carolina after the retreat weekend, Hanna contacted a Chinese pastor who then invited the couple to a Chinese Bible study. Later, the pastor was able to lead the man to Christ.

Five Hindus attended one retreat session. One had become a Christian and gave his first public testimony of his conversion that weekend as the other four Hindus listened. "There are no words to describe how wonderful it is to know Christ," he said.

We thank the Lord for this outreach to the world. We not only have individual students coming here, but also international church groups. Greater Atlanta has become such a cosmopolitan center that its residents now speak 130 different languages. Muslim mosques and Hindu temples have risen in this Bible-belt city.

Among the new immigrants are many Christians who have formed their own churches. Some of them are coming to us for Spiritual Life retreats. We have had Spanish, Liberian, Nigerian, Cambodian, Korean, Iranian and others. We hope to enlarge that number.

We have a tremendous commission from the Lord and wonderful opportunities. There are many American congregations that have used our facilities through the years. But there are churches that have not been able to come because of our lack of sleeping space and the general inadequacy of some of the buildings. The old summer-camp-style buildings we inherited with the property over twenty years ago have been fixed, renovated, painted, and pampered. We feel that there is not much more one can do with these deteriorating buildings.

The challenge before us is huge—to see the Lord provide the lodge and conference center we have been envisioning for twenty long years. We have the architect and the plans drawn up. Now you can see why we were so excited about the coming of Glynn and Deborah Galloway to spearhead the urgently needed building program. The cabin by the lake is just the first step. From that site we can see the forested ridge where the lodge will rise one day. It is like the challenge Caleb faced in his old age. But he was not daunted by the prospect of standing up to giants in order to gain his mountain. He dared to call out to the Lord, "LORD, GIVE ME THIS MOUNTAIN!!"

In January of 2001 we made this same cry, "Lord give us this mountain!!" We had very little in the way of resources. We lacked funds, strength, materials, and workers. We could also identify with Caleb in our ages as a staff. Most of us were in the retirement-age bracket. Our eldest was eighty-six and still heavily involved. Yet, we have the same Spirit Caleb had. He was strong in the Lord and so he dared to confront a mountain full of giants when he was eighty-five, for the Lord gave him the same strength and vigor he had when he was a youth. And

Lord, Give Us This Mountain!!

so we follow on hard after the Lord, eager to see Him fulfill His plan for us and for Fellowship Valley Retreat. We firmly believe His promise . . . WITH GOD ALL THINGS ARE POSSIBLE!!

Engineer, Lewis Canup, architect, Tom Gregory, staff man, Gary Hedwall, and road builder, John Yearwood, study the area where the new driveway to the Lodge will be built.

Builder Glynn Galloway, working on the roof of the new cabin.

      We thank the Lord for a gift of $5,000 given by a new brother in Christ. It was for the purchase of the windows and doors for the cabin!
      A dear friend in California caught the vision of helping to outfit the bedrooms and sent thirteen sets of sheets and pillow cases for the beds, as well as towels and wash cloths for the retreat guests who will use the cabin. How we thank the Lord for these who come along side to help!

Gary Hedwall and Dick Linder, assisting with cabin construction.

Putting roof sheeting on the cabin.

Bonnie, Alline, and architect Tom Gregory, looking at the plans for the lodge.

Larry Walker, from the Environmental Health Department, and architect Tom Gregory, study the lodge site area.

The log residence which will house two families.

The beautiful lakeside gazebo

Dick Linder with two Nigerian men who attended a men's retreat.

Gary Hedwall with his new Haitian friend. Special meetings are held for the children of the international students also.

An Iranian pastor baptizing one of the members of his Congregation in our lake.

A Cambodian church holding a service at the lakeside.

Steve Cowart baptizing a Russian student in our lake.

Dick Linder with a group of men from a Spanish church retreat.

A group of students from the Philippines.

Bonnie Hanson, with a Chinese lady who attended the student weekend session.

Shari Hedwall, our head bookkeeper.

Mavis Linder with five Chinese students who came to Christ during a student retreat.

Alline Marshall with Chinese students.